RORSCHACH LOCATION
AND SCORING
MANUAL

RORSCHACH LOCATION AND SCORING MANUAL by Leonard Small, Ph.D., Director, Special

Research, Vocational Advisory Service, New York City; Consulting Psychologist, Altro Health
and Rehabilitation Service, New York City; Instructor, New York University.

GRUNE & STRATTON, Publishers   NEW YORK and LONDON   1956

Library of Congress Catalog Card No. 55-10398

Copyright 1956
Grune & Stratton, Inc:
381 Fourth Avenue
New York 16, N. Y.

Printed and bound in U. S. A.

INTRODUCTION

A graphic and convenient system for locating on the cards of Rorschach's test any one of the many details and combinations of details eliciting a response from a subject has long been needed. S. J. Beck has established areas on each card, defined in terms of the frequency with which they elicit responses. This manual presents graphically those widely used categories, with a thumb-index for instant reference. In addition it assembles more than 6,000 responses scored by Beck and 17 other Rorschach workers.

The manual thus is designed to expedite Rorschach *scoring* by:

(1) permitting quick location of scoring areas without reference to text;

(2) presenting more than 6,000 responses scored for area, determinant and content;

(3) listing + and − responses alphabetically in the same column;

(4) offering a thumb-index to location chart for each card;

(5) giving Z-activity scores at hand for each card;

(6) combining the scoring experience of 18 Rorschach workers including Beck, Klopfer, Rorschach, Oberholzer and Rickers-Ovsiankina.

The experienced Rorschacher will not need this warning, but the student and beginner is cautioned against using this manual to score responses in a mechanical and rigid manner. The material offered here is a guide to the scoring experience of leading workers, but can not be a substitute for the careful inquiry which is a mainstay of Rorschach procedure.

The manual also offers an aid to *instruction and study* of the test, in that the graphic presentation and the systematizing of a body of experience can be expected to foster both comprehension and review.

INSTRUCTIONS

The procedure used in this manual is based upon Beck's* scoring areas and scoring method.

THUMB-INDEX: The index on the right margin is the guide to the location chart and responses for each card.

LOCATION CHART: Each area is separately presented in a solid black drawing, with the surrounding area indicated by a broken line.

The legend at the bottom of each drawing identifies the area by number and refers to the page on which the responses for the area are listed. Page references for W responses are carried in a box at the top of each location chart. Page references for DW, DdW and certain Atypical responses are listed at the right of each location chart. Above these appear the Z-activity scores for the card.

SCORING: *Area*. The usual notations—W, D, Ds, Dd, Dds—are indicated at the bottom of each area drawing. They also appear at the head of each listing of responses, and at the top of each succeeding page to which responses for the area are carried over.

Determinant. This is scored to the left of each response. The + or − signs appearing alone refer to the F quality. All other determinants are scored with M, the usual C combinations, and Beck's symbols, V, Y, T. Sometimes accurate determinant scoring by an author was not available, throwing the burden upon the individual examiner's inquiry. In such cases the reader's attention is called to possibilities for determinant-scoring by various notes in brackets within the body of the response, *e.g.*, [may be M], [may involve T], [C?], [Y?]. The scoring of all authors has been converted to Beck's symbols for consistency.

Content. Content is scored to the right of each response, with Beck's categories and abbreviations.

Populars. The popular responses appear in solid capital letters. Only Beck's populars are used because of their statistical foundation. Populars of other authors which do not coincide with Beck are not indicated as popular.

---

*Beck, S. J.: Rorschach's Test, I—Basic Processes. New York: Grune and Stratton, 1950.

Position. Directional carats appear above the first letter of the response. No sign is used if the only position is ∧. The directional carats frequently demonstrate the logic of the scoring. In some cases the response is P if seen from one approach but is not P if seen from another direction; in other instances F is + in one position and − in another aspect of the same area.

Variations and Special Conditions. These are contained within brackets in the body of the response.

SOURCES: The basic sources are the published volumes of S. J. Beck and a mimeographed scoring compilation by Maria Rickers-Ovsiankina, entitled "Rorschach Scoring Samples."

The names of the Rorschach workers whose scorings are compiled here are underscored in parentheses after each response. The following abbreviations are used:

Be	Beck, S. J.
Bi	Binder, H.
Bl	Bleuler, M.
Bo	Boss, M.
Du	Dubitscher, F.
Ga	Gardner, G. E.
He	Hertz, M. R.
Kl	Klopfer, B.
Lo	Loepfe, A.
LU	Loosli-Usteri, M.
Ml	Mueller, M.
Mu	Munz, E.
Ob	Oberholzer, E.
Oe	Oeser, O. A.
RO	Rickers-Ovsiankina, M.
Ro	Rorschach, H.
Vi	Veit, H.
Ve	Vernon, P. E.

ATYPICAL RESPONSES: Where feasible these follow the regular listing of responses for the area (e.g., in card I, an atypical response is based upon Dds 29 with adjacent Dd and is listed following the regular responses to Dds 29). Atypical responses which could not be placed with such logic are presented in special sections referred to on the location charts.

ACKNOWLEDGMENTS

I am especially indebted to my friend and colleague, Leopold Bellak, M.D., for his participation in the exchange of ideas that led to the development of this manual, and for his help and encouragement during its preparation. Nancy D. Larson can not adequately be thanked for the Herculean job of indexing, collating and manuscript preparation she has performed so well and so cheerfully (nor can she be blamed for errors, since final editing responsibility remains mine). I am grateful to Professor Mary Blade of Cooper Union School of Engineering for her assistance in the preparation of the location chart drawings and to Martin Weihrauch for his inking of my pencil sketches. My wife's contributions I can not even list because of their number and their relationship to every phase of this work.

L. S.

RORSCHACH LOCATION
AND SCORING
MANUAL

Dds 32 . . p. 17

Dds 29 . . p. 16

Dds 30 . . p. 17

Dd 31 . . . p. 17

Dd 25 . . . p. 15

Dds 26 . . . p. 16

Dd 27 . . . p. 16

Dd 22 . . . p. 15

any or all

Dd 23 . . . p. 15

Dd 24 . . . p. 15

D 7 . . . p. 13

D 8 . . . p. 13

D 9 . . . p. 14

D 4 . . . . p. 9

D 5 . . . . p. 12

D 6 . . . . p. 12

D 1 . . . p. 6

D 2 . . . . p. 7

D 3 . . . p. 8

Sign	Item	Code
+	airplane (Be)	Tr
+	angel [may be M] (Be, LU)	H, Rl
M+	angel and two goblins (Ro)	H, Rl
+	animal, marine (Be)	A
+	animal, prehistoric (Be)	A
+	animal, sea (Be)	A
-	animal split open (Be)	A
+	arms in costume (Be)	Hd, Cg
M+	arms in supplication, in some costume (Be)	Hd, Cg
+	art, Chinese [may be Ws] (Be)	Art
+	BAT (Be, Ga, Ob, Ro)	A
-	bats, two (Be)	A
-	bear (Be)	A
+	beetle (Be, Bl)	A
+	being, flying [may be M+] (Ro)	A
+	bird (Be, Ga, Ro)	H
-	body, human (Be)	A
-	bomb, new-fashioned (Ro)	H
+	bomber (Be)	Im
+	bone, skeletal (Be)	Tr, Im
		An
+	bug (Be)	A
+	bug squashed (Be)	A
+	building, Chinese (Bo)	Ar
FY+	building, gloomy (Bi)	Ar, Ab
-	building with cupola (Du)	Ar
+	BUTTERFLY (Be, Ga, Ob, Ro, Vr)	A
+	cap, auto radiator (Be)	Art, Tr
+	∨ carving, stone [may be Ws] (Be)	Mn, Art
+	characters, mythological (Be)	H, My
-	∨ chest (Be)	Hd
+	children (Be)	H
FY-	cloud formations (Bo)	Cl
YF	cloud in sky (Du)	Cl, Na
+	clouds (Be)	Cl
-	clown (Be)	H
+	coat-of-arms (Be, He)	Art
+	crab (Be, Bl)	A
+	cross section, biologic (Be)	An, Sc
+	cross section, brain [may be Ws] (Be)	An, Sc
+	∨ cross section, Chinese bronze [may be Ws] (Be)	Art

+	cross section, spinal cord (Be)	An, Sc
+	cross section through vertebra (Mu)	An, Sc
+	˅crown [may be Ws] (Be, Mu)	Art
M+	dancers, two (Be)	H
+	design (Be)	Art
+	diagram (Be)	Art
-	dinosaur (Be)	A, Sc
-	dish, fancy (Be)	Hh
FY+	dish, fruit, ornamented with fruit [in the black] (Bo)	Hh, Bt
+	dragon (Be)	A, My
-	dragon-fly (Be)	A
+	dragon, flying (Du)	A, My
+	drawing, experimental (Be)	Art
Y+	drawing in black and white (Ro)	Art
+	eagle (Be)	A
+	eagle on crest or seal [any art form of eagle] (Be)	A, Art
+	eagle, spread [U.S. symbol] (Be)	A, Art
+	emblem (Be, He)	Art
M+	Erl-King with child in his cloak (Ro)	H, My

+	face, cat's [Ws] (Be)	Ad
+	face, false (Be)	Hd?, Rc?
+	face, tiger's (Be)	Ad
+	figure, nightmare (Be)	H, Ab
+	figurehead (Be)	Art
M+	figures, two, big, with coat floating in the wind, standing at a basin (Ro)	H, Cg
-	flower (Be)	Bt
+	flowers around goblet (Bo)	Bt, Hh
-	fly (Be)	A
-	font, holy water (Bi)	Rl
-	˅football player [may be M] (Be)	H, Rc
+	fossil on stone (Be)	Mn, Sc
+	fountain with angels (Be)	Ls, Art
M+	giants, two, pulling two dwarfs who raise hands imploringly (Mu)	A, My
+	girls [may be M] (Be)	H
-	governor on motor (Be)	Im
+	˄˅hat (Be)	Cg
FY+	hat, Chinese, of gray tulle (Bi)	Cg
+	head (LU)	Hd

I – W cont'd

-	head, animal's (Be)	Ad
-	head, bull's (Be)	Ad
-	head, cow's (LU)	Ad
-	head, rabbit's (Be)	Ad
-	head, ram's (Be)	Ad
+	^v helmet (Be)	Aq
+	insect (Be)	A
YF	iron work (Kl)	Art?, Ar?
-	jacket with sleeves (LU)	Cg
Y	lace (Kl)	Pr?, Hh?
+	landscape and reflection (Be)	Ls
-	leaf (Be, Bo)	Bt
-	leaf, torn (Be)	Bt
+	lion, winged, in fountain (Be)	A, Ls
+	lobster (Be)	A
M-	^v man with legs apart (Be)	H
+	map, raised (Be)	Ge
+	^v map, topographic (Be)	Ge
-	marine growth (Be)	A?, Bt?
+	mask [Ws] (Be, Bo)	Hd?, Rc?
-	^v mask (Be)	Hd?, Rc?

M+	men, two, swearing something on altar (Ro)	H, Rl
+	monster, fairy-tale, four-eyed [probably Ws] (Be)	A, My
+	^v monument (Be, LU)	Art
FY	moose on edge of lake with his reflection in the lake (Kl)	A, Ls
+	MOTH (Be)	A
+	mountains (Be)	Ls
+	ornament (Be)	Art?, Pr?
+	owl sitting on tree (Be)	A, Bt
+	^v pagoda, Japanese (Be)	Ar
+	pattern, lace (Be)	Pr?, Hh?
-	pelt, spread out (Ob)	A
+	pelvis (Be, Ga, Mu)	An
+	people, two [may be M] (Ga)	H
+	photgraph (Be)	Photo
+	picture (Be)	Art
+	rock formation (Be)	Ls
-	rocks (LU)	Ls
-	ship (Be)	Tr
+	show window decorations: coat, corsage, draperies (Ro)	Ar, Cg

+	skeleton, bird's [may be Ws] (Be)	An
+	skeleton, outline of (Be)	An
+	sketch, charcoal (Be)	Art
+	ˇskull, animal's [may be Ws] (Be)	An
-	ˇskull, no eyes, no features, just bone structure [not including white space] (Be)	An
+	sky, clouded (Be)	Na, Cl
-	snowflake under microscope (Be)	Sc
-	sponge (Be)	Hh?, A?
YF	stalagmites (Bi)	Mn, Na
+	statue, Egyptian (LU)	Art, Ay
+	stencil (Be)	Im
+	swallow (Be)	A
YF	swamp with holes [may be Ws] (Bi)	Ls
+	thistle with leaves (Bo)	Bt
-	thorax (Bl)	An
+	tie clasp, woman's (Be)	Pr
+	totem pole form (Be)	Ay
-	tree (Be)	Bt
+	ˇturban (Be)	Cg

+	ˇurn, Japanese (Be)	Hh
+	vampire (Ro)	A
+	vertebra, outline of (Be, Bl, Ga)	An
-	wasp (Be)	A
+	witches, two (Be)	H, My
M+	woman, dancing, flare in dress (Be)	H
FY+	x-ray, bone structure (Be)	An
FY+	x-ray, chest (Be)	An
FY+	x-ray, crab (Be)	An
FY+	x-ray, insect (Be)	An
FY+	x-ray, lobster (Be)	An
+	x-ray plate [scored F- when the specific anatomy detail would be F-, e.g., lungs] (Be)	An
FY+	x-ray, ribs (Be)	An

I-D1

+	antlers (Be)	Ad
-	boulders [may be FV-] (Be)	Ls
+	claws (Be)	Ad
+	claws, lobster's (Be)	Ad
-	collar of woman's dress (Be)	Cg
+	coral (Be)	A
+	crab (Be)	A
+	crustacean sucking fingers (Be)	Ad
+	feelers (Be)	Ad
+	fingers (Be)	Hd
-	∨ fish (Be)	A
-	fork and spoon '(Be)	Hh
+	∧∨ hands (Be)	Hd
M+	hands grasping for something (Ro)	Hd
+	∧∨ hands with mittens on (Be)	Hd, Cg
-	head, animal's (Be)	Ad
+	head, duck's (Be)	Ad
+	heads, birds' (Be)	Ad
+	hills (He)	Ls
+	horns, beetle's (Be)	Ad
+	horns, deer's (Be)	Ad

+	horns, elk's (Be)	Ad
+	mandibles (Be)	Ad
+	∧∨ mittens (Be)	Cg
+	nipper, crayfish's (Be)	Ad
+	pincers (Be)	Ad
+	pincers, animal's (Lo)	Ad
+	pincers, beetle's (Bo)	Ad
-	sticks (Be)	Bt
-	teeth (Be)	Hd
-	uvula (Ro)	An

ATYPICAL
D 1, with Dd 22

+	crab (Be)	A
-	genitalia, female (Be)	Hd, Sex
+	head, deer's (Be)	Ad
+	insect (Be)	A
+	lobster (Be)	A
-	vulva (Be)	Hd, Sex

6

+	angel [s] [may be M] (Be)	H, Rl
+	animal (Be)	A
+	˅ animal, mythological (Be)	A, My
-	bear [s] (Be)	A
+	bears turning around (Ro)	A
+	birds fighting (Be)	A
+	birds, perching, conventionalized (Be)	A, Art
+	brontosaurus (Be)	A, Sc
-	butterfly (Be)	A
+	cliff (Be)	Ls
YF	cloud, thunder-storm (Bi)	Cl
+	clouds (Be)	Cl
+	crows, snapping (Ro)	A
+	˅ donkey (Be)	A
-	dragon (Be)	A, My
M+	duelists (Ro)	H
+	elephant [D 8 is ear] (Be)	A
+	face [outer edge of D 2 as pro-file, D 8 as long nose] (Be)	Hd
+	figure [s], winged, human (Be)	H
+	girls, Chinese [may be M] (Be)	H
+	girls, dancing [may be M] (Be)	H
M+	goblins, two, with brooms under arms (Ro)	H, My
FY+	grimace, devil's (Bi)	Hd, Ab
+	˅ gryphon (Be)	A, My
+	human, any class [may be M] (Be)	H
-	lungs (Be)	An
+	man [may be M] (Be)	H
+	map (Be)	Ge
FY+	map, relief (Be)	Ge
+	men [may be M] (Be)	H
+	mountain, or part of (Be)	Ls
-	newspaper rack (Be)	Im
+	Pegasus (Be)	A, My
M+	policeman, flying (Be)	H
+	rock (Be, LU)	Ls
+	Russians, two [may be M] (Be)	H
+	Santa Claus [may be M] (Be)	H, My
+	scarf (He)	Cg
-	sea-horse (Be)	A
+	sky [as clouds] (Be)	Na

I – D 2 cont'd

+	ˇstones (Be)	Mn
–	ˇstones, prehistoric [similar to arrowheads] (Be)	Aq, Im
+	stork (Be)	A
+	trees (Be, LU)	Bt
Y	waves, the play of (Bi)	Ls
+	wing[s] (Be)	Ad
+	witches [if flying is M+] (Be)	H, My
M–	wolf, dancing (Be)	A
M+	women bending backwards (Ro)	H

ATYPICAL
upper half of D 8

–	cat, flying (Be)	A
–	fox (Be)	A
M+	woman sitting (Be)	H

both D 2 with Dds 32

–	ˆhalf-moon (Be)	As

in D 2, just interior to D 9, two dark spots as eyes, adjacent spot as nose

+	bear, teddy (Be)	A, Rc

+	cat ´(Be)	A
+	elephant (Be)	A

I – D 3

+	aqueduct of Sylvius (Be)	An, Sc
+	BODY, BABY'S [may be M] (Be)	H
+	BODY OR FORM, HUMAN [may be M] (Be)	H
+	body, woman's, one-half (Be)	Hd
+	chalice (Be)	Rl
+	CHILD [may be M] (Be)	H
+	cord, spinal, frog's (Be)	An, Sc
+	crocodile lying on belly (Ro)	A
+	ˇemblem, Girl Scout pin (He)	Art
M+	figure, diabolic, with hanging hands (Ro)	H, Ab
+	FIGURE MILITARY [may be M] (Be)	H
+	FORM, FEMALE [may be M] (Be)	H
+	LADY WITHOUT DRESS [may be M] (Be)	H
+	legs (Be, Ro)	Hd
+	LEGS, CHILD'S (Be)	Hd

+	medulla (Be)	An, Sc
+	midbrain (Be)	An, Sc
-	penis (Be)	Hd, Sex
+	PERSON [may be M] (Be)	H
+	person, half (Ro)	Hd
+	scarab (Be)	Ay
FY+	SILHOUETTE OF WOMAN'S BODY (Be)	H
+	statue (Be)	Art
+	vase (Be, Ro)	Hh

ATYPICAL
D 3 with adjacent Dd, including Dds 26

-	skeleton (Be)	An

I - D 4

+	alligator (Be)	A
+	animal (LU)	A
-	bear (Be)	A
-	bee (Be)	A

+	beetle (Be, Bl)	A
+	body [may be M] (Be)	H
+	body, double (Be)	H
+	body, female (Be)	H
+	body, female, without head, breasts protruding (Ro)	Hd
+	body, headless [may be M] (Be)	Hd
+	body, insect's (Be)	A
+	body with one pair of limbs and two torsos [may be M] (Be)	H
+	brain-stem (Be, Bl)	An, Sc
-	branch (He)	Bt
+	bug (Be)	A
-	cat (Be)	A
-	caterpillar (Be)	A
+	child (Be, LU)	H
MY+	clown with outstretched arms, a ghostly figure (Bi)	H, Ab
-	cord, spinal, area of human (Be)	An, Sc
-	cow (Be)	A
+	crab (Be, LU)	A
+	cup (He)	Hh

+	˅cup, stone, on a gravestone (He)	Art, Dh
M+	Dalai Lama sitting (Ob)	H, Rl
M+	dancers, women (Be)	H
M+	danseuse (Ro)	H
-	dog (Be)	A
+	elves (Be)	H, My
MY+	figure, half human and half demon, threateningly holds its hands up (Bi)	H, Ab
+	figure, human [may be M] (Be)	H
M+	figure, woman's with tightly pressed together legs (Ro)	H
-	fly [with Dds 26] (Be)	A
+	˅glass (He)	Hh
+	goddesses [may be M] (Be)	H, My
+	gnome [may be M] (Be)	H, My
+	˅goblet with foot (Bo)	Hh
+	gymnastic apparatus (Be)	Im, Rc
+	hour-glass (He)	Aq
+	human, any form [may be M] (Be)	H
+	humans, two [may be M] (Be)	H
+	insect (LU)	A
+	ladies, Spanish [may be M] (Be)	H

+	lobster (Be)	A
+	man [may be M] (LU)	H
+	medulla (Be)	An, Sc
+	men, two [may be M] (Be)	H
-	monument (Be)	Art
-	mountain (Be)	Ls
+	nuns [may be M] (Be)	H, Rl
-	owl (Be)	A
+	people, two [may be M] (Be)	H
M+	priest praying, oriental (Be)	H, Rl
+	scarab (Be)	Ay
-	scorpion (Be)	A
+	shield (Be)	Aq
-	silkworm (Bo)	A
-	skeleton (Be)	An
+	skeleton in light wrapping (Ob)	An
+	skeleton, something from (Lo)	An
+	sphinx (Be)	Art, Ay
+	spider (Be)	A
-	spine, human (Ro)	An
-	tree (Be, He)	Bt

I — D 4 cont'd

+	∧∨ urn (Be)	Hh
+	∧∨ vase (Be, He)	Hh
-	violin (Be)	Mu
+	woman [may be M] (Be, LU)	H
M+	woman, frightened (Ro)	H, Ab
M+	women, two, sport ladies (Ro)	H, Rc
+	x-ray (Be)	An

ATYPICAL
upper part of D 4 with Dds 30

+	∨ bridge in goldfish bowl (Be)	Ar

lower half of D 4

+	∨ figure, human [usually quaint, usually sitting, e.g., Buddha; may be M] (Be)	H

lower half of D 4 with Dds 26

+	mask (Be)	Hd?, Rc?
+	pumpkin (Be)	Bt

upper half of D 4

+	armor, suit of (Be)	Aq

+	bowl (He)	Hh
+	chest, person's, where it comes together (He)	An
+	crab (Be, Mu)	A
-	crater (Be)	Ls
-	faces, deer's (Be)	A
+	gate (He)	Ar
+	haystack (He)	Ru, Bt
+	head, beetle's (Ro)	Ad
-	head, owl's (Be)	Ad
+	hills (He)	Ls
+	lobster (Be)	A
-	monkey (Be)	A
-	pelvis (Be)	An
M+	people kissing (Be)	H
+	skeleton, part of (He)	An
+	throat, part of (He)	An

upper half of D 4, with lower two thirds of D 4.

+	∨ lantern, Japanese (Be)	Hh

I-D5

−	comb, rooster's (Be)	Ad
+	ear (LU)	Ad
+	face, man's (Be)	Hd
+	face, wolf's (Be)	Ad
+	hat (Be, He)	Cg
+	head [s], bear's (Be, Ro)	Ad
+	head, dog's (Be)	Ad
+	head, fox's (Be)	Ad
+	head, human [any kind or class, e.g., cardinal] (Be)	Hd
+	head, Indian's (Be)	Hd
−	head, parrot's (Be)	Ad
−	jaw, bear's (Be)	Ad
−	paw (LU)	Ad
+	peninsula (He)	Ge
+	profile (Be)	Hd
+	fox [only when D 8 is head or muzzle] (Be)	A
+	wolf [only when D 8 is head or muzzle] (Be)	A

I-D6

+	bust of man (Be)	Hd, Art
+	celery (Be)	Bt
−	crown (Be)	Art
+	˅ flower (He)	Bt
+	hay, bunch of (Be)	Ru, Bt
−	head, dog's (Be, RO)	Ad
+	heads, human [or of special class, e.g., child, Negro] (Be, RO)	Hd
+	hypophysis (Be)	An, Sc
+	shocks, wheat (Be)	Ru, Bt
+	tree [usually ˅] (Be)	Bt

ATYPICAL
D 5 with D 8

−	animal [when accent is on D 8 as tail] (Be)	A
+	dog [only when D 8 is head or muzzle] (Be)	A

I-D7

–	animal [when accent is on D 8 as tail] (Be)	A
+	bird [s] (Be)	A
+	dog (Be)	A
+	eagle (Be)	A
+	head, dog's (Be)	Ad
+	wolf (Be)	A

I-D8

–	anvil (Be)	Im, Vo
–	arrow (Be)	Im
–	bird with beak (Be)	A
–	broom (He)	Hh
+	cliff, stone (Be)	Ls
–	cloud (Be)	Cl
–	∨ dog [entire animal] (Be)	A
+	drapery (Be)	Hh
–	∨ face, human (Be)	Hd
+	faces, animals' (Be)	Ad

–	fin, shark's (Be)	Ad
–	flint (Be)	Aq
+	gargoyles (Be)	Art
–	head, alligator's (Be)	Ad
+	head, dog's (Be, Bl)	Ad
–	head, horse's (Ro)	Ad
–	∨ head, Indian's (Be)	Hd
+	head with hood (Ro)	Hd, Cg
+	head with tiara (Ro)	Hd, Pr
+	head, wolf's (Be)	Ad
–	horn [s] (Be)	Ad
–	isle, coral (Be)	Ls
–	leaf (He)	Bt
–	map (He)	Ge
–	∨ map of South America (He)	Ge
+	mountain (Be)	Ls
+	nose, fox's (Be)	Ad
+	rock (Be)	Ls
+	>< sail (He)	Tr, Rc?
+	seal (Be)	A

+	∨ stone (He)	Mn
–	thigh (Be)	Hd
–	tree (Be)	Bt
–	∧ tree (He)	Bt
–	umbrella (Be)	Im
+	umbrella, opened halves of (Ro)	Im
+	wing, airplane (Be)	Tr
+	wing[s], bat's (Be, Ro)	Ad
+	wing [s], bird's (Be)	Ad
+	wing [s], butterfly's (Be)	Ad
+	wings, Mercury's (Be)	Hd, My

ATYPICAL
D 8 with adjacent Dd

–	turkey (Be)	A

I – D 9

+	cliffs (Be)	Ls
+	∧∨> face, dog's (Be)	Ad
+	face, human (Be, RO)	Hd
+	face, monkey's (He)	Ad
+	head, cat's (Be)	Ad
+	∨ head, human (Be)	Hd
FY+	head, kitten's, with light and dark fur, spotted (Bi)	Ad
+	head, lion's (Be)	Ad
–	head, monkey's (Be)	Ad
+	heads, animals' (Be)	Ad
+	rocks (Be)	Ls
+	shrubs (He)	Bt

I - Dd 22

+	boulders [may be FV+] (Be)	Ls
+	buttocks (Vi)	Hd, Sex
+	haystack (He)	Ru, Bt
+	heads (Be)	Hd
+	heads, monkeys' (Be)	Ad
+	hills [may be FV+]	Ls
-	humps, camel's (Be)	Ad
+	labia (Be)	Hd, Sex
+	lips (Be)	Hd
+	mountains [may be FV+] (Be)	Ls
-	rectum (Be)	An, Anal
-	testicles (Be)	Hd, Sex

I - Dd 23

+	airplane (Be)	Tr
+	insects (Be)	A
+	islands (Be)	Ls
+	musical notes (Be)	Mu

-	owl (Be)	A

I - Dd 24

+	bell (Be)	Mu
-	hour-glass (Be)	Aq
+	shield [crest] (Be)	Aq, Art

I - Dd 25

+	animal (Be)	A
-	cliff (Be)	Ls
+	face (Be)	Hd
+	face, animal's (Be)	Ad
+	gnome (Be)	H, My
+	head, old man's (Be)	Hd
+	pig (Be)	A

J - Dds 26

+	bird (Ro)	A
+	carvings (Be)	Art
+	eyes, four (Be)	Hd?, Ad?
+	glaciers (Be)	Na
+	kite (Ro)	Rc
+	lakes (Lo)	Ls
+	mask details (Be)	Hd?, Rc?
+	puzzles [cutout] (Be)	Rc
+	seas (Ro)	Ls
−	triangles (Ro)	Im?
+	ventricles (Be)	An
+	windows (Be, Oe, Ro)	Ar
+	wings, airplane (Be)	Tr
+	wings, butterfly's (Be, Ro)	Ad
−	wings,,fly's (Be)	Ad

ATYPICAL
Dds 26 with interspace

+	butterfly (Be)	A
+	face, human (Be)	Hd

I - Dd 27

+	belt buckle (Be)	Cg?, Pr?
+	canal, central (Be)	An, Sc
−	heart, human (Be)	An

I - Dds 29

+	mouth, pumpkin's, for Halloween (Be)	Bt, Rc
−	triangle (Be)	Im?
+	wings, butterfly's (Be)	Ad

ATYPICAL
Dds 29 with adjacent Dd

+	wings, airplane (Be)	Tr

16

I - Dds 30

-	arms doubled up (Be)	Hd
-	gloves (Be)	Cg
-	head, rooster's (Be)	Ad
-	London bobby (Be)	H
-	rectangle (Be)	Oj

I - Dd 31

+	brain, rat's (Be)	An, Sc
+	clam, part of (RO)	Ad
+	cord, spinal, piece of (Be)	An
+	cup, stone (He)	Art
+	feet (Be)	Hd
+	v flower part (He)	Bt
+	v head, dog's (Be)	Ad
-	organ, sex, female (Ro)	Hd, Sex
-	organ, sex, male (Ro)	Hd, Sex
-	phallus (Be)	Hd, Sex
+	snout, crocodile's (Lo)	Ad
-	snout, fish's (Ro)	Ad
+	v stone, cemetery (He)	Art, Dh
-	tail (LU)	Ad
-	tail, cat's (Be)	Ad
-	tail, lizard's (Be)	Ad

I - Dds 32

+	archway (He)	Ar
+	bay (He)	Ls
+	bridge (He)	Ar
+	canyon [may be V] (Be)	Ls
YF.VF	plateau, covered with snow and ice, lost in distance (Bi)	Na
+	water (He)	Ls

I - DW

-	mountains (Bo)	Ls

D 1

+	arms in costume (Be)	Hd, Cg

D 1 with D 8

+	butterfly (Be)	A
-	wasp (Be)	A

D 8

+	bird (Be)	A

I - DdW

Dd 27

+	arabesque (Be)	Art, Ar

Dd 27 with Dds 26

+	beetle (Be)	A
+	face, false (Be)	Hd?, Rc?
-	island of sea (Be)	Ls

I - ATYPICAL D

upper half entire

+	airplane (Be)	Tr
+	emblem [bird form] (Be)	Art
-	head, fox's (Be)	Ad

upper half excluding D 8

-	x-ray, pelvis (Be)	An

upper half excluding D 8 but with Dds 32

v	bridge (Be)	Ar
-	lamp (Be)	Hh

lower half entire

v	crown with jewels (Be)	Art, Mn
-	pelvis (Be)	An
-	prow, ship's (Be)	Tr

W excluding D 7

+	beetle (Be)	A
+	bug (Be)	A
+	butterfly (Be)	A

+	stingray (Be)	A

W excluding D 8

+	pelvis (Be)	An

I - ATYPICAL Dd

midline Dd

+	spine (Be)	An

outer edge outline Dd, various sectors

+	coast with bays (Be)	Ls
+	map [may be of specific coastal place] (Be)	Ge
+	shore, lake (Be)	Ls
+	shore line (Be)	Ls

lighter Dd exterior to D 3

+	dress, thin (Be)	Cg

lower edge Dd of D 8

-	face (Be)	Hd

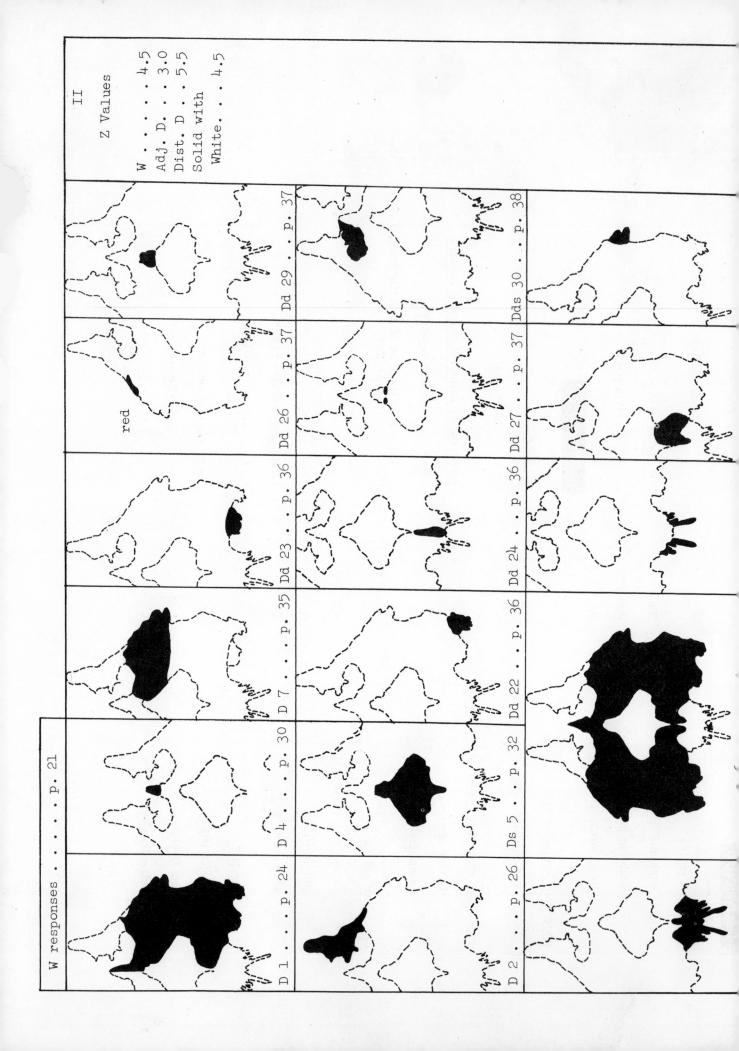

II

Z Values

W 4.5
Adj. D . . . 3.0
Dist. D . . 5.5
Solid with
White . . . 4.5

W responses . . . . p. 21

D 1 . . . p. 24   D 4 . . . p. 30   D 7 . . . p. 35   Dd 23 . . p. 36   red   Dd 29 . . p. 37

D 2 . . . p. 26   Ds 5 . . p. 32   Dd 22 . . p. 36   Dd 24 . . p. 36   Dd 26 . . p. 37   Dd 27 . . p. 37   Dds 30 . . p. 38

II - w

FC-	anemone, sea (Be)	A
+	anatomy, general [insides, organs] (Be)	An
FC-	animal, sea (Be)	A
+	animals (Ga)	A
M+	animals with paws together (Ga)	A
M+	bears, boxing (Be)	A
+	bears, two, in coat-of arms turned toward each other, no faces, but with caps on (Mu)	A, Art
+	bears, two, without heads (Du)	Ad
-	beetle (Ob)	A
-	biologic, something (Be)	Sc
FC-	bird, foreign summer (Bl)	A
-	body, human, opened up (Be)	An
-	body, person's (LU)	H
M+	BUFFOONS, TWO, CARNIVAL (Ro)	H
-	bug (Be)	A
+	∧∨ butterfly (Be, Ro)	A
FC+	butterfly, beautiful (Bl)	A
M+	CLOWNS, TWO (Ob)	H
M+	CLOWNS, TWO, DANCING TOGETHER (Ro)	H

+	cord, spinal, section of (Be)	An, Sc
-	cords, vocal (Be)	An
CF+	crab [color emphasized] (Bl)	A
-	crab, horseshoe (Be)	A
-	creature (Be)	A
+	cross section [s], brain (Be)	An, Sc
M.CF+	DERVISHES, ARABIAN, WITH TURBANS (Be)	H
+	decoration (LU)	Art
+	DEVILS (Be)	H, Rl
+	diagram (Be)	Art
-	dog, strange (LU)	A
M+	dogs, two, young, balancing something on their noses (Ro)	A
FC+	drawings, impressionistic (Be)	Art
CF	exploding bullet, pieces flying apart, fire (Bo)	Fi
CF+	exploding kerosene lamp (Ro)	Fi
+	explosion (Be)	Fi
-	figure, plant (Ro)	Bt
+	∨ figures, two, grotesque, in tableaux [if human figures, score M and P] (Be)	H?, A?

Score	Response	Codes
CF	fire of splintering bullet (Bo)	Fi
CF+	flame and smoke (Be, Mu)	Fi
+	flower (LU)	Bt
-	∨ flower-pot (Be)	Hh
M-	∨ football player kneeling, rear view (Be)	H, Rc
FC-	formation, fantastic (Du)	Ab
M+	GAME, SUCH AS "PEAS PORRIDGE HOT" (Be)	H, Rc
-	heart shape (Bo)	Art?, An?
CF	Hell with two devils; at bottom, hell fire; at top, flames (Bo)	Rl, Fi
+	HUMANS [any class, nationality, vocation, or condition; may be M] (Be)	H
C	ink mixed with blood (Bo)	Blood
-	insect (Be)	A
+	insides (Be)	An
+	JAPANESE [may be M] (Be)	H
CF+	lobster [color emphasized] (Bl)	A
-	lobster, opened (Be)	A, An
M.CF+	MAGICIANS, TWO, DANCING, WITH RED CAPS (Bl)	H, Cg
-	map (Be)	Ge
+	MASKERS [may be M] (Be)	H
-	∨ men [may be M] (Be)	H
M.CF+	MEN, TWO, WITH RED CAPS, TURKS (Bl)	H, Cg
FY+	monument, stone or granite; marble would be smoother (Be)	Art, Mn
+	moth, fire (Be)	A
+	nervous system, central (Be)	An, Sc
CF+	nervous tissue section; red spots show disintegration (Be)	An, Sc
+	organism, primitive (Be)	Sc
+	organs (Be)	An
CF+	painting (Be)	Art
CF	painting, futuristic (Bo)	Art
-	pelvic girdle (Be)	An
FC-	pelvic region; lateral red are kidneys, center red is the opened testicles (Bo)	An, Sex
-	pelvis, human (Ro)	An
M+	PEOPLE (Ga)	H
FV+	PERSON ON ICE, WITH IMAGE REFLECTED IN THE ICE (Be)	H, Na
M+	PERSONS, TWO (Ro)	H
M+	PERSONS, TWO, PRAYING (Ro)	H, Rl

CF.Y	war picture, bursting bullets on night terrain (Bi)	Fi
+	WITCHES [may be M] (Be)	H, My
+	WITCHES, TOY [may be M] (Be)	H, Rc
M+	WOMEN KNITTING (Ro)	H
-	x-ray, spinal vertebra (Be)	An

M+	PRIESTS, TWO, PRAYING (Mu)	H, Rl
M+	PRIZE FIGHTERS (Be)	H, Rc
M.CF+	SANTA CLAUSES PLAYING "PEAS PORRIDGE HOT" [where color is emphasized] (Be)	H, Rc
CF-	sealing-wax, burning, with two burning drops (Bo)	Fi
M.Y+	silhouette, dancing bears' (Be)	A
M.Y+	silhouettes, animals', two, licking at each other with the tongues (Bo)	A
CF+	smoke and flame (Be, Mu)	Fi
+	statues (Be)	Art
M+	STUDENTS, INTOXICATED (Be)	H
-	sun in eclipse (Be)	Ls
-	tooth (Be)	Hd
+	top [toy] within a black spot [Ws] (Bo)	Rc
+	toys, Christmas (Be)	Rc
-	vagina (Be)	An, Sex
+	vertebra (Du, Ga)	An
-	vertebra with hole in it [Ws] (Bl)	An
+	volcano (Be)	Ls

II - D 1

−	∨animal (Be)	A
+	∧animal (Be)	A
+	animals with forepaws raised against each other [this is not M] (Be)	A
+	ape (Be)	A
+	bear [s] [if D 7 is head score P] (Be)	A
−	∨∧bird (Be)	A
+	bison (Be)	A
−	boat (Be)	Tr
+	body, beast's (Be)	A
+	buffalo (Be)	A
+	bull [s] (Be)	A
+	bulldogs [if D 7 is head score P] (Be)	A
MC+	bulldogs, standing at a fire [if D 7 is head score P] (Be)	A, Fi
−	calves [when D 4 is muzzle] (Be)	A
+	calves [when Dd 31 is muzzle] (Be)	A
+	cat (Be)	A
−	clouds (Be)	Cl
+	∨clown [may be M] (Be)	H

+	cow [s] (Be)	A
+	cub [s] (Be)	A
FY−	curtain, dark (Be)	Hh
−	∨dog (Be)	A
+	∨dog [s] [if D 7 is head score P] (Be)	A
FY+	dog, black poodle [if D 7 is head score P] (Be)	A
+	dog, toy [if D 7 is head score P] (Be)	A, Rc
+	dogs, facing each other [if D 7 is head score P] (Be)	A
+	elephant [s] (Be)	A
−	embryo (Be)	An, Sc
−	fish (Be)	A
−	grass (Be)	Bt
−	guinea-pigs (Be)	A
+	heads, dogs' (Be)	Ad
−	lamb [s] [when D 4 is muzzle] (Be)	A
+	lamb [s] [when Dd 31 is muzzle] (Be)	A
−	lions (Be)	A
+	man, any class [with or without inclusion of D2 as hat; may be M] (Be)	H

D V cont'd

−	map (Be)	Ge
−	monkey)Be)	A
+	mountain (Be)	Ls
+	nervous tissue, with degenerated area (Be)	An
−	pelt [s] (Be)	A
M+	people [in some action or stance: fighting, kneeling, looking, praying, talking] (Be)	H
+	pig (Be)	A
+	puppies [if D 7 is head score P] (Be)	A
+	rabbit (Be)	A
+	rhinoceros (Be)	A
+	rock [as mountain] (Be)	Ls
+	sheep [when Dd 31 is muzzle] (Be)	A
−	skeleton (Be)	An
+	skin, animal's (Be)	A
−	tree trunks (Be)	Bt
YF−	tree trunks, black (Be)	Bt
+	wings (Be)	Ad

ATYPICAL
D 1 with D 2

−	boar, wild (Be)	A
M+	CLOWNS (Be)	H
+	HUMANS, ANY CLASS [may be M] (Be)	H
+	MASKERS [may be M] (Be)	H
+	WITCHES [may be M] (Be)	H, My
+	WOMEN [may be M] (Be)	H

both D 1 with D 4

−	calves sucking bottle [this is not M] (Be)	A

edge of D 1

+	map contour (Be)	Ge

horizontal streaks in D 1 (scored Dd)

+	ribs (Be)	An

Dd in D 1 near D 4 (scored Dd)

FV	mountains, and hills in back, very indistinct (Be)	Ls

-	andirons (Be)	Hh
+	animal [when specifically named; most small species, except a few, like squirrel, which are -] (Be)	A
-	animals, large [except a few of primitive form, such as hippopotamus, which are +] (Be, Ga, Ob)	A'
-	bird (Be)	A
-	birds, two (Ro)	A
-	bison (Be)	A
C	blood (Be)	Blood
CF+	blood blotches (Be)	Blood
CF+	blood splashed (Be)	Blood
-	bonfire (Be)	Fi
-	body tissue (Be)	An
+	brownie, caricature of (Bo)	H, My
-	bug (Be)	A
-	bull (Be)	A
+	butterfly [ies] (Be)	A
+	cap (Be)	Cg
FC+	cap, liberty, of French Revolution (Be)	Cg

FC+	cap, Santa Claus' (Be)	Cg
+	cat [s] (Be)	A
CF-	cells, body, eosin stained (Be)	An, Sc
+	centaurish (Be)	My
-	chickens (Be)	A
-	cocoon, silk (Ro)	Ad
CF-	comb, turkey's (Be)	Ad
+	cowboy [may be M] (Be)	H
+	creature, animated [may be M] (Be)	A
CF+	devil [s] (Be)	H, Rl
+	dog, any variety (Be)	A
+	dragons (Be)	A, My
-	duck with fur coat on (Be)	A, Cg
+	dwarfs (Be)	H, My
+	dwarfs, decorative, like one finds in a flower garden (Bo)	H, Art
M+	dwarfs, two, moving toward each other (Ro)	H, My
-	England (Be)	Ge
-	face, camel's (Be)	Ad
+	faces [may be M] (Be)	Hd

+	figure, impish [probably M since "impish" implies action] (Be)	H	+	hats, stocking (Be)	Cg
+	fire (Be)	Fi	+	head [s] (Be, Ro)	Hd
C	fire, grass on (Oe)	Fi	+	head, antelope's (Ro)	Ad
-	fish (Be)	A	-	head, dog's (Be)	Ad
CF	flames, two (Ro)	Fi	-	head, horse's (Lo)	Ad
-	flower (Be)	Bt	+	headdress, Oriental, detail of (Be)	Cg
+	ᵛfoot, human (Be)	Hd	M+	hippopotamus dancing (Be)	A
-	foot, human (Be, Ro)	Hd	-	hooves (Be)	Ad
-	foot, lobster's (Be)	Ad	-	ᵛhuman (Be)	H
+	form, human (Be)	H	+	kewpies (Be)	H, Rc
+	fox (Be)	A	+	lantern, Japanese (Be)	Hh
C	ᵛglow of evening (Lo)	Na	+	ᵛlegs (Be, Lo)	Hd
-	goat (Be)	A	-	legs (Be)	Hd
+	gremlins (Be)	H, My	-	lion (Be)	A
+	hams, two (LU)	Fd	-	lungs (Be)	An
-	hand, with greatly enlarged finger (Ro)	Hd	+	mannikins (Be)	H?
-	hands (Be)	Hd	+	marmots, two little (Ro)	A
+	hares, March (Be)	A	+	mask (Be)	Hd?, Rc?
+	hats, any variety (Be)	Cg	+	men [may be M] (Be)	H
			+	monster [s], ancient (Be)	A, My

II – D 2 cont'd

−	organs, inner (Be)	An	
−	penis (Be)	Hd, Sex	
−	phallic symbol (Be)	Ab, Sex	
−	pillar (Be)	Ar	
+	proboscis, shellfish's (Be)	Ad	
+	rabbit [s] (Be)	A	
+	^v seals (Be)	A	
+	v shoe and stocking (Ro)	Cg	
−	slide, microscope (Be)	Sc	
+	snail (Be)	A	
+	v South America (Be)	Ge	
−	squirrel (Be)	A	
+	squirrels (Ro)	A	
−	stockings (Be)	Cg	
+	v>< stockings, any [e.g., Christmas] (Be, Kl)	Cg	
−	thumbs (Be)	Hd	
−	thumbs, sticking up [this is not M] (Be)	Hd	
−	tongue (Be)	Hd	
−	torches (Be)	Im	
+	turban (Be)		Cg
−	turkey (Be)		A

ATYPICAL
See D 1 Atypical on Page 25.

Dd projecting from D 2

+	cigarette (Be)		Oj
+	tongues sticking out (Be)		Hd

Score	Response	Category
–	anemone, sea (Be)	A
–	beetle (Be)	A
–	bird (Be)	A
C	blood (Be, Ro)	Blood
CF+	blood splotches (Be)	Blood
CF	blood from vagina of woman (Bo)	Blood, Sex
CF+	blood splashed (Be)	Blood
C	bonfire (Be)	Fi
–	big (Be)	A
FC+	BUTTERFLY (Be, Ga, Ro)	A
FC+	butterfly, rear part of (Ro)	Ad
+	buttocks [or variation of, sometimes with Dds] (Be)	Hd, Sex
–	coral formation (Be)	Ls
–	crab (Be)	A
–	creature, marine (Be)	A
+	crystal, snow (Be)	Na
–	daddy-longlegs (Be)	A
+	darning, needle [insect] (Be)	A
–	devil (Be)	H, Rl
CF+	dogs breathing fire (Be)	A, Fi

Score	Response	Category
CF+	explosion (Be)	Fi
C	fire (Be, Bl)	Fi
–	fish (Be)	A
C	flame (Be)	Fi
CF+	flame, little (Be)	Fi
–	flower (Be, LU)	Bt
M–	girl, Ziegfeld, with arms (Be)	H
+	head, fox's (Lo)	Ad
–	head, lobster's (Be)	Ad
–	heart (Be)	An
CF–	heart, bleeding (Be)	Rl, Blood
–	heart, form of (Bo)	An
CF–	Heart, Sacred, bleeding (Be)	Rl, Blood
C	ink, red (Mu)	Im
+	insect (Be)	A
CF–	lobster, red, as if cooked (Be)	A, Fd
–	mask (Be)	Hd?, Rc?
C	menstruation (Be)	Blood, Sex
+	MOTH (Be)	A
+	organ, genital, female [any description of is +] (Be)	Hd, Sex

FC+	organ, sex, woman's [the red is partially responsible for the interpretation] (Bi)	Hd, Sex
CF	raspberry sauce (Mu)	Fd
+	rectum (Be)	An, Anal
+	ˇ"sexual" (Be)	Ab, Sex
-	stand, artist's (Be)	Vo
CF	sun, half of (Ro)	Ls
CF+	ˇ sun, rising or setting (Be, Lo)	Ls
CF+	torches with wicks (Be)	Fi
-	unicorn (Be)	A, My
CF	volcano (Lo)	Ls

ATYPICAL
D 3 with adjacent black Dd

+	anus and buttocks (Be)	Hd, Anal
CF+	fireplace (Be)	Fi, Hh
CF-	ˇ marine floor with seaweed (Be)	Ls, Bt
-	ˇpeacocks, two (Be)	A

II - D 4

+	arrow, arrowhead (Be)	Im
-	backbone, decayed part of (Bi)	An
+	beak, bird's (LU)	Ad
-	beak, eagle's (Be)	Ad
-	bone (Be)	An
-	bottle (Be)	Hh
-	brain, rabbit's (Be)	An, Sc
-	Buddha (Be)	H, Rl
+	building (Be)	Ar
-	candle (Be)	Hh
+	can opener (Be)	Hh
+	castle (Be)	Ar
+	cement stopper (Be)	Im
+	clippers (Be)	Im
-	clitoris (Be)	Hd, Sex
+	cornucopias (Be)	Hh
-	Crucifixion (Be)	Rl
+	dagger (Be)	Im
+	ˇdelta, river (Be)	Ls
+	dome, building (Be)	Ar
+	drill (Be)	Im

II — D 4 cont'd

	Item	Code		Item	Code
−	face, lizard's (Be)	Ad	FY−	ribbon, black (Be)	Pr
+	forceps (Be)	Im, Vo	+	roof (LU)	Ar
−	glasses [vessel] (Be)	Hh	+	scissors (Be)	Im
+	hands (Be)	Hd	+	shears (Be)	Im
−	hat (Be)	Cg	−	slippers (Be)	Cg
−	head (Be)	Hd	−	snake, coiled (Be)	A
−	head, bird's (Be)	Ad	−	snout, pig's (Be)	Ad
+	head, gargoyle's (Be)	Art	+	spear (Be)	Im
−	headdress, Egyptian (Be)	Ay	FV+	stair, distant (Ro)	Ls
+	house (Be)	Ar	+	steeple, church (LU)	Ar, Rl
+	instrument, surgical (Be)	Im, Vo	−	sword (Be)	Im
+	lancet (LU)	Im, Vo	−	tail (Be)	Ad
−	man (Be)	H	+	temple (Be)	Ar, Rl
+	monument (Be)	Art	−	Tibetan, back view (Be)	H
−	mountain [Pike's Peak] (Be)	Ls	+	topknot, animal's (Be)	Ad
+	pen, fountain (Be)	Im	+	tower (Be, Lo)	Ar
−	penis (Be, Ro, Vi)	Hd, Sex	+	tree, fir (Be, Bi, Bo)	Bt
−	penis, dog's (Be)	Ad, Sex	−	tree, palm (Be)	Bt
+	pliers (Be)	Im	+	tree [s], pine (Be)	Bt
+	pyramid (Be, LU)	Ar, Ay	−	unicorn (Be)	A, My
+	reamer, pipe (Be)	Im	−	uterus (Be)	An, Sex

II – D 4 cont'd

-	wishbone (Be)	An

ATYPICAL
grey Dd in D 4 (scored Dd)

-	legs, lady's (Be)	Hd

D 4 with Ds5

FV+	castle and gate, walking up to (Be)	Ls, Ar
+	lamp (Be)	Hh
+	tornado with funnel (Be)	Cl

D 4 with Ds 5 and D 3

+	torch (Be)	Im

D 4 with upper half of D 6

-	eagle (Be)	A

-	airplane (Be)	Tr
FY+	anemone, white (Bi)	Bt
+	basket, hanging (Be)	Hh
-	bat (Be)	A
-	beet (Be)	Bt
-	bell (Be)	Mu
-	bellows (Be)	Im
-	boat (Be)	Tr
-	body, girl's, part of (Be)	Hd
+	bottle, glue (Be)	Hh
+	bouquet, flower (Bo)	Bt
+	bowl for lamp (Be)	Hh
-	building, modern (Be)	Ar
+	chandelier (Be)	Hh
+	cover, pottery (Be)	Hh
M-	dancer, ballet (Be)	H
-	dress, flare-y, old-fashioned (Be)	Cg
FV+	entrance, cave (Be)	Ls
FV+	entrance, tunnel (Be)	Ls
+	fissure in rock (Be)	Ls
+	gate (Be)	Ar

II – Ds5 cont'd

	Response	Loc.	Code
+	globe, electric light (Be)		Hh
−	hat, Malay (Be)		Cg
+	heart (LU)		An
+	hole, hell hole (Be)		Ab
−	kite (Be)		Rc
+	lake (Be)		Ls
FV+	lake seen from distance (Be)		Ls
+	lamp (Be)		Hh
+	lampshade (Ro)		Hh
+	lantern, Japanese (Be)		Hh
−	mask (Be)		Hd?, Rc?
−	meadow and pond (Bo)		Ls
+	pond (Be)		Ls
+	promenade (Be)		Ls
YF+	road, a large park, surrounded by five dark trees (Ro)		Ls, Bt
YF+	road in bright sun (Bi)		Ls
−	rocket (Be)		Rc?
M.Y+	silhouette of woman who holds up her apron with both hands lest one see her head (Bo)		H, Cg
−	stingray (Be)		A

	Response	Code
−	stomach (Be)	An
+	top [toy] (Be, Bo)	Rc
−	tree, Christmas (Be)	Bt, Rc
+	vase (Be)	Hh
FV+	walk (Be)	Ls
+	water, body of (Be)	Ls

ATYPICAL

Ds 5 with D 1

	Response	Code
V	depth, because of grey things (Be)	Ab

Ds 5 with D 3

	Response	Code
+	Volcano (Be)	Ls

Ds 5 with Dds 29

	Response	Code
FV+	promenade, walking up through flight of stairs (Be)	Ls

Score	Response	Content
FY+	> animal, big, totally black (Bi)	A
-	bat (Be, Ro)	A
+	bears, two (Ro)	A
M+	bears, two, dancing (Ro)	A
-	bird (Be)	A
-	body, human, interior of (Be)	An
+	bones, hip (Vi)	An
+	butterfly (Be)	A
FY	cloak, black, blown by wind (Kl)	Cg
+	clouds (Be)	Cl
YF	clouds, two, black (Kl)	Cl
+	coccyx, ending of (Du)	An
YF	cotton, black (Kl)	Oj
+	cross section, brain-stem (Be)	An, Sc
+	fireplace (Be)	Hh
+	^v heads, two animals' (Ro)	Ad
+	heads, two sheep's (Ro)	Ad
-	insect, winged (Be)	A
-	lungs, lobes of (Ro)	An
M+	man, drawing head into collar, getting ready to curse (Ro)	H, Cg
-	map of New York State (Be)	Ge
-	map of United States (Be)	Ge
M+	> men, two, running away, holding their legs together (Lo)	H
M+	> monks, two, who kindle fire while they are dancing (Ro)	H, Rl
YF	> mountain crest, threatening. Dark crevices down into valley (Bi)	Ls, Ab
+	muffs, two (Ro)	Cg
FC-	nerve cells (Du)	An, Sc
+	pants, two pairs, women's (Ro)	Cg
+	pelvis (Be, Ga, Ro)	An
+	rabbits without heads (Bo)	Ad
FY-	raven, big, flying (Bi)	A
+	ribs [or similar chest anatomy when Dd streaks are ribs] (Be)	An
FY	rock slate (Vi)	Mn
-	rug (Be)	Hh
-	rug, bear (Be)	A, Hh
-	sows, two (Ro)	A
YF	swamp, muddy, in which dark things are swimming around (Bi)	Ls
FY-	women in dark cloaks (Bi)	H, Cg

II – D 6 cont'd

`II – D 7`

ATYPICAL
emphasis on red Dd

CF-	back, person's, bones and blood (Be)	An, Blood
CF-	bat, wounded (Be)	A, Blood

D 6 with Ds 5

+	land with pond (Be)	Ls
FV+	opening, cave (Be)	Ls
+	pelvic girdle (Be)	An
-	platform on top of well (Be)	Ar
-	shell, crab (Be)	Ad

+	dog (Be)	A
+	head, animal's (Be)	Ad
+	*head, ape's (Be)	Ad
+	head, dog's (Be)	Ad
+	*head, dracula's (Be)	Hd
+	*head, horse's (Be)	Ad
+	*head, Indian's (Be)	Hd
+	*head, monkey's (Be)	Ad
-	head, poodle's (Be)	Ad
+	*head, sheep's (Be)	Ad
-	head, turtle's (Be)	Ad
-	head, whale's (Be)	Ad
+	*profile, ape's (Be)	Ad
+	*profile, monkey's (Be)	Ad

*face or muzzle must be at Dd 31 to be scored +

II - Dd 22

	Response		
+	chicken (Be)	A	Fi
+	˅ faces (Be)	Hd	Rc
+	feet, bear's (Be)	Ad	An
-	head, dog's (Be)	Ad	Rc
+	head, man's [or any specifically named individual, e.g., King Lear] (Be)	Hd	Hd
+	˅ man, old, of the mountain (Be)	Hd	Hd, Sex
+	man with roughed-up hair (Bl)	Hd	Ab, Sex
M+	˅ profile whistling (Be)	Hd	H, Cg

ATYPICAL
Dd 22 with Dd 23

	Response		
+	coast, like Greece (Be)	Ge	Ab, Sex

II - Dd 23

	Response		
+	head, Indian's (Be)	Hd	An, Sex
+	head, old man's (Be)	Hd	H
+	˅ mountain (Be)	Ls	

II - Dd 24

	Response		
CF+	˅ beacon on building (Be)	A	Fi
-	bowling pin (Be)	Hd	Rc
+	discharge system (Be)	Ad	An
-	dumbbell (Be)	Ad	Rc
-	face (Be)	Hd	Hd
+	genitalia, female (Be)	Hd	Hd, Sex
-	˅ penis symbol (Be)	Hd	Ab, Sex
-	person with scarf [may be M] (Be)	Hd	H, Cg
+	"sexual" (Be)	Hd	Ab, Sex
+	vagina (Be)		An, Sex
-	woman [may be M] (Be)	Ge	H

ATYPICAL

	Response		
+	˅ anal region (Be)	Hd	Hd, Anal
+	anus, horse's (Be)	Hd	Ad, Anal

Dds in Dd 24

	Response		
C	blood (Be)	Ls	Blood
+	bones, cheek (Be)		Hd
+	bridge (Be)		Ar
+	diamond (Be)		Mn

II - Dd 25

+	antlers (Be)	Ad
-	candlesticks (Be)	Hh
-	crystal [s] (Be)	Mn
+	feelers, insect's (Be)	Ad
+	horn [s], unicorn's (Be)	Ad, My
+	icicle [s] (Be)	Na
-	spears (Be)	Im
-	stalagmites (Be)	Mn, Na
-	sword (Be)	Im
-	tails, lobsters' (Be)	Ad
-	tusk, elephant's (Be)	Ad

II - Dd 26

+	caterpillar (Be)	A
+	mouse (Vi)	A
CF	neck, bleeding (Bo)	Hd, Blood
+	sunset (Be)	Ls
> +	tail, furry (Be)	Ad

II - Dd 27

+	bridge (Be)	Ar
+	locks, canal (Be)	Ls

II - Dd 28

+	buttock [s] (Be)	Hd, Sex

ATYPICAL
tiny Dd on inner edge of Dd 28

M	man sitting in armchair (Be)	H, Hh

II - Dd 29

+	dome (Be)	Ar
+	flask (Be)	Hh
+	pot (Be)	Hh
Y.T.	water, clear, because it is smooth (Be)	Ls

II - Dds 30

–	chicken (Be)	A
–	embryo (Be)	An, Sc

II - Dd 31

+	beak, bird's (Be)	Ad
–	claw [s], lobster's (Be)	Ad
+	crag, mountain (Be)	Ls
+	head (Bo)	Hd
+	head, animal's (Bl)	Ad
+	head, dog's (Be)	Ad
+	head, turtle's (Be)	Ad
+	∧∨ man, old, of the mountain (Be)	Hd
+	mouth, fish's (Be, Lo)	Ad
+	profile, human (Be)	Hd
+	profiles, animals' (Be)	Ad
FY+	silhouette, camel's mouth (Be)	Ad

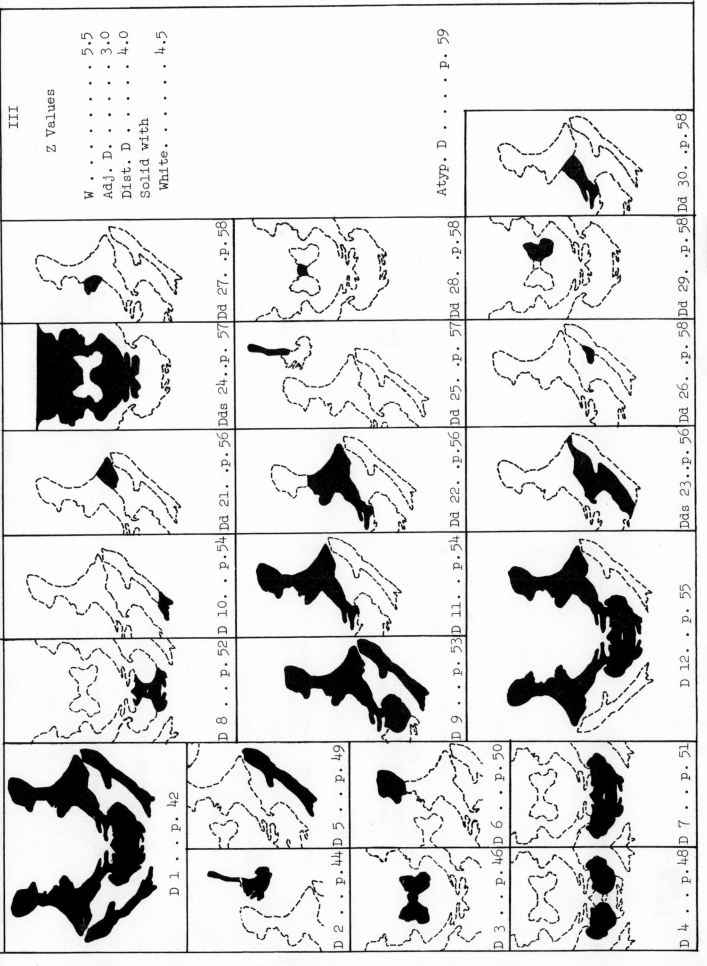

+	animal, sea [ink fish] (Du)	A
CF	body, human, drawing of ; reds are regions of greatest blood congestion (Bo)	An, Art
-	brain section with nerve centers [may be FC-] (Be)	An, Sc
+	ˇbumblebee, magnified (Be)	A
FC-	butterfly (Ob)	A
+	caricatures, two [may be M] (Bo)	H, Art
Cn	colors, three, with the paper: white, black and red. The same colors only in other shape (Ro)	Color
+	ˇcyclops [may be M] (Be)	H, My
TF.YF	dampness, impression of, because the color is that of clouds, dry, black ones (Oe)	Cl
M+	dance or something like that, twins as trade-marks on knives (Mu)	H
M+	ˇdanseuses, two, who are throwing legs up in the air (Du)	H
+	design, conventional [may be FC+] (Be)	Art
+	drawing, modernistic [may be FC+] (Be)	Art
M+	fauns or human beings, they have horse feet (Be)	H, My

+	figures, two, human [not seen in motion] (Ro)	H
-	flower-like something [may be FC-] (Ro)	Bt
+	ˇfly (Be)	A
+	ˇfrog (Be)	A
+	gorilla (Be)	A
+	ˇgrasshopper (Be)	A
+	head, gnat's, magnified (Ro)	Ad
+	heraldry symbol (Be)	Art
+	inkfish [probably involves Y] (Du)	A
-	map (Be)	Ge
M+	"mashers" [dudes] who bow and greet each other (Ob)	H
M+	men in full dress, two, holding receptacles (Ro)	H, Cg
M+	monkeys, two, play (Ro)	A, Rc
-	pelvis (Be)	An
+	pelvis (Ga)	An
M+	people (Ga)	H
M+	people in motion (Ga)	H
+	picture puzzle (Be)	Rc
+	ˇpraying-mantis (Be)	A

III — W cont'd

FY+	urn, grave — one would have to ignore all details and consider only the black color. Inside is the hollow space of the urn (Bi)	Dh
-	⌄vase with short legs, associated with aspidistras (Oe)	Hh
M+	waiters, two, holding receptacles (Ro)	H
M+	woman, old, washwoman or something like that, holding up her hands [the feet of the men ordinarily perceived are the arms of the woman; the body of the woman is formed by the two men figures, including all the white parts between] (Ro)	H
M+	puppets, two (Ro)	H, Rc
-	satyr from waist down (Be)	Hd, My
M+	scribes, two, holding council (Ro)	H
MY+	shadow of figures, crouched — kind of death dance — skeleton with black bones. The figures have a male sex organ, but a female breast. A death dance of hybrids, which is very mad (Bi)	H, Sex
+	⌄skeleton, human (Be)	An
FY+	sketch done in shadows [may be YF+] (Be)	Art
FC+	somebody with automobile spectacles and red tie [may be M] (Bl)	H, Cg
-	spider (Be)	A
M+	theater, new, such one can lift free in the air [catatonic speech mannerism] (Ro)	H
+	⌄tomcats, two, which turn away from each other, look at their tails; and, if one wants to be nasty, one could say that they a are dropping something [red lateral] (Mu)	A, Anal
FY+	⌄trees, stunted, dry, in the twilight (Bi)	Bt, Ls

+	acrobats [the arms are interpreted as legs; not seen in motion] (Ro)	H
−	animal [s] (Be)	A
−	bears, teddy, two [may be M] (Be)	A, Rc
+	birds, large, when resembling human form [may be M] (Be)	A, H
+	bodies, framework of (Be)	An
+	˅cannibal [may be M] (Be)	H
M+	CANNIBALS OVER POT (Be)	H
+	CARTOONS [may be M] (Be)	H, Art
+	chicken (Be)	A
+	CHILDREN [may be M] (Be)	H
+	cocks, fighting (Be)	A
M+	COITUS, MAN AND WOMAN IN (Be)	H, Sex
+	˅crab (Oe)	A
FY+	cloud formation (Bo)	Cl
M+	DANCE, SILLY (Be)	H
M+	˅dancers (Be)	H
+	DOLLS OF BLACK SATIN [may be M] (Be)	H, Rc
M+	DOLLS, TWO, FACING EACH OTHER, PERFORMING SOME SORT OF DANCE (Be)	H, Rc
+	Donald Duck [may be M] (Be)	A, H
M+	duck carrying satchel (Be)	A, H
M+	FIGURES, BENDING FORWARD (Be)	H
+	FIGURES, GROTESQUE [may be M] (Be)	H
M+	FIGURES, GROTESQUE, FACING EACH OTHER, HOLDING SOMETHING BETWEEN THEM (Be)	H
M+	FIGURES, OR PEOPLE, DISTORTED, BENDING AND HOLDING SOMETHING BETWEEN THEM (Be)	H
M−	FIGURES, SITTING [the arms are seen as the legs] (Ro)	H
+	FIGURES, STAGE [may be M] (Be)	H
−	frog [s] (Be)	A
M+	GAME WHERE YOU HOLD HANDS AND GO AROUND IN A CIRCLE (Be)	H, Rc
?	head, fly's, with big eyes (Oe)	Ad
+	HUMAN [any form or class of, e.g., men, children, grotesque figures, Siamese twins; also representations of humans as jumping jacks, marionettes, stage figures. The varieties named are endless; may be M. The card must be ∧ for P] (Be)	H

+	human [content, usually, cannibal; men, the bodies in pieces; Negro, primitive – or variation; Negresses dancing; may be M] (Be)	H
M+	JUMPING JACKS (Be)	H, Rc
-	lambs (Be)	A
M+	MAN, WHO HOLDS ARMS UP AND HAS HEAD, IN EGYPT ON THE PYRAMIDS (Bo)	Hd, Ar
-	map (Be)	Ge
M+	MARIONETTES (Be)	H, Rc
+	MEN [may be M] (Be)	H
+	men, the bodies in pieces (Be)	H
+	Men, two [may be M] (Ro)	H
M+	MEN, TWO, EACH CARRYING BASKET: MEETING AND BOW-ING (Be)	H
-	monkey [s] (Be)	A
M+	Negresses, dancing (Be)	H
+	Negro, primitive [may be M] (Be)	H
+	ostriches (Be)	A
+	pelvis, human (Du)	An
FV+	PERSON AND REFLECTION (Be)	H
+	rooster fight (Be)	A
+	skeleton [s] (Be)	An
+	sketch, incomplete (Be)	Art
FY-	smoke (Be)	Fi
+	toy, Christmas (Be)	Rc
+	TWINS, SIAMESE [may be M] (Be)	H
+	WOMEN, TWO WITH HATS ON, BENDING FORWARD (Be)	H, Cg
FY+	x-ray, bones (Be)	An

Code	Entry	Category
+	ameba (Be)	A, Sc
FC+	anemone, sea (Be)	A
+	∧∨≷∡ animal [the animal may be falling, lying, diving, flying, or in other posture] (Be)	A
+	animal, dream (Be)	A
+	animal in motion (Ga)	A
+	animals, dogs, looking back on their tails (Ro)	A
+	animals, fantastic, resembling dogs (Ob)	A
-	ape (Be)	A
FC-	artery and lung (Be)	An
+	bagpipe, Scotch (Be)	Mu
+	bear, young, but with leg like goat's (Ro)	A
+	< beggar, one-legged [may be M] (Be)	H
+	∧> bird [s] (Be, Ga)	A
CF-	birds, young, who fall out of nest, because they are so red (Bo)	A
C	blood (Be)	Blood
CF+	blood splotches (Be, Ob)	Blood
-	butterfly [may be CF- or FC-] (Be)	A
+	cat (Be)	A

Code	Entry	Category
CF+	cat, red, falling through air (Be)	A
+	∧< chickens (Be, Ga)	A
FC-	clowns, two [may be M] (Ro)	H
-	club [s] (Be, LU)	Im
-	cocoon (Be)	Ad
-	cord, umbilical [may be FC-] (Be)	An
FV+	creature, flying (Be)	A
M+	∨ creatures, fairy, bent by wind (Be)	H, My
M+	dancers, toe (Be)	H
+	dandelion (Be)	Bt
+	decoration, stage [probably a color response] (Be)	Art
Y+	∨ dejection (Be)	Ab
+	devils [may be CF+ or FC+; may be M] (Be)	H, Rl
+	dipper (Be)	Hh
+	∧∨> dog, twisting, running, jumping (Be, Ro, Mu)	A
-	dragon (Be)	A, My
+	dwarfs (Be)	H, My
+	elf [elves] (Be)	H, My
FC+	embryo, human (Be)	An

FC+	embryos, drawing of (Bo)	An, Art
FC+	esophagus and stomach (Be)	An
FV+	figures, angel, in churches, where one sees the angels approach flying (Bo)	H, Rl
+	figures, impish [may be M] (Be)	H
C	fire (Be)	Fi
FC+	flower (Be)	Bt
CF	flowers, funeral, red of, which are drooping from the urn (Bi)	Bt, Dh
-	fork (Be)	Hh
+	Fox terrier (Ro)	A
+	gargoyles (Be)	Art
+	germ under microscope [may be FC+] (Be)	Sc
+	ˇgirl [may be M] (Be)	H
M+	girl, dancing (Be)	H
+	gnome [may be M] (Be)	H, My
FV-	goats leaping through air (Be)	A
+	gremlins [may be M] (Be)	H, My
-	hat with string (Be)	Cg
+	head, horse's, of chess game (Ro)	Ad, Rc
+	horse (Be)	A
-	insects (Be)	A
-	instrument, musical, like violin (Be)	Mu
FC-	intestines (Be)	An
-	islands, two (Be)	Ls
FC+	kidney with ureter (Be)	An
-	lightning flashes [may involve C and V] (Be)	Fi
+	lion with long tail (Be)	A
FC-	lung and artery (Be)	An
FC-	lungs (Be)	An
+	man [may be M] (Be)	H
-	meat, cuts of [may be FC-] (Be)	Ad
+	monkeys, squatting (Ro)	A
+	^ˇmonkeys, two, hanging (Be)	A
+	nerve process [may be FC+] (Be)	An, Sc
-	ostriches (Be)	A
+	paramecium (Be)	A, Sc
FC+	^ˇparrot on pole (Be, Bo)	A
FC+	parrots, two (Ro)	A
M+	performers, trapeze (Be)	H
+	ˇplant bent by wind (Be)	Bt

III – D 2 cont'd

+	poodle, little, with long tail and head turned (Bl)	A
+	portieres (Be)	Hh
+	puppets [may be M] (Be)	H, Rc
-	question marks, two (Be)	Al
-	rabbits (Be)	A
-	rat [s] (Be)	A
-	reservoir, dammed, with inlet and side arms (Bo)	Ls
FC+	rooster (Be, Bo)	A
+	sea-horses (Be)	A
-	seaweed (Be)	Bt
+	stomach [may be FC+] (Be, Ga)	An
+	tree [s], palm (Be)	Bt
FC+	˅turkey (Be, Bo)	A
-	venison hanging from hook [may be FC-] (Be)	A
-	violin (Be)	Mu
+	wig (LU)	Pr

ATYPICAL
D 2 with D 3

C	blood (Be)	Blood

III - D 3

+	backbone, section of (Be)	An, Sc
+	˅barrier (Be)	Ls
-	bird (Be)	A
+	bird, summer (Bl)	A
-	bivalve (Be)	A
C	blood (Ob)	Blood
+	bone (Be)	An
+	bones, hip (Be)	An
+	bones, pelvic (Be)	An
FC+	BOW, RED (Be, Ga)	Cg
+	BOW-KNOT (Be)	Im
-	brassiere (Be)	Cg, Sex
+	brassiere, corset (Ro)	Cg, Sex
+	˄˅butterfly [may be CF+ or FC+] (Be, Ga)	A
+	cloak on chair (Be)	Cg, Hh
-	coccyx (Be)	An
+	cord, spinal, piece of (Be)	An, Sc
-	dumbbell (Be)	Rc
+	ears (LU)	Hd
-	ear warmers (Be)	Cg

46

−	eyeglass (Be)	Im
CF	flowers, funeral, red of, which are drooping from the urn (Bi)	Bt, Dh
−	fly (Be)	A
+	gray matter of spinal cord (Be)	An, Sc
FC−	gum of mouth (Be)	An
FC−	hearts, two, conventionalized (Be)	Art
FC−	hearts, two, in the middle (Bo)	An?
−	insect (Be)	A
+	kidney [s] [may be FC+] (Be, Bo)	An
−	lambs (Be)	A
CF−	larynx with two pieces of meat hanging on it (Bo)	An
CF+	lung [s] (Be)	An
−	mask (Be)	Hd?, Rc?
+	moth (Be)	A
FC−	mouth, roof of (Be)	An
−	mustache (Be)	Hd
+	necktie [may be FC+] (Be)	Cg
−	pants hanging on clothesline (Be)	Cg
−	protector, athletic (Be)	Cg, Sex
+	ribbon (Be)	Pr

FC+	ribbon, hair, in barrette (Be)	Pr
FC+	ribbon, hair, made of satin (Kl)	Pr
−	skeleton, parts of (Be)	An
CF−	sky, red (Be)	Na
+	sponge, bathing, tied together in the middle (Bo)	Hh
−	thorax (Be)	An
FC+	TIE, BUTTERFLY, MODERN (Ro)	Cg
FC+	TIE, RED (Be)	Cg
−	truss (Be)	Oj
+	wings, water (Be)	Rc
+	ᴠ wings, butterfly, abdomen missing [may be FC+] (Be)	Ad
−	wishbone (Be)	An
CF−	women, redheaded (Be)	H

	Item	Code
+	bags (Be)	Hh
+	basket [s] (Be)	Hh
+	bones, pelvic (Ga)	An
-	boots (Be)	Cg
-	buffalo, small (Be)	A
-	cases, violin, two, distorted (Ob)	Mu
-	caterpillars (Lo)	A
-	chickens (Be)	A
+	child [ren] (Be)	H
+	˅cubs, bear (Be, Ro)	A
-	cups (Be)	Hh
-	dog, any (Be)	A
+	embryo (Be)	An
+	face, human (Be)	Hd
FY+	fan, feathered (Be)	Pr
-	feet, human (Be)	Hd
+	gloves, boxing (Be)	Rc
+	gourds, water (Be)	Hh
+	hats (Be)	Cg
-	˅head, animal's (Be)	Ad
-	head, elephant's (Be)	Ad
+	˅head, human, large-skulled [or person named specifically] (Be)	Hd
FY	˅head, Negro's, with typical hair visible in outline and shading (Kl)	Hd
+	head, skeleton's (Be)	An
+	heads, cannibals' (Be)	Hd
+	˅heads, Negroes' (Ro)	Hd
+	hedgehog (Ro)	A
-	hen (Be)	A
-	kidney (Be)	An
+	lamps, Chinese (Be)	Hh
-	lung [s] (Be)	An
M+	man, little, stooping down (Ro)	H
+	mice (Ro)	A
-	mountains (Be)	Ls
+	muffs (Be)	Cg
+	mushrooms (LU)	Bt
+	package or something like that (Mu)	Oj
+	porcupines (Be)	A
+	'possum (Be)	A

	Response	Code		Response	Code
+	pot [s] (Be)	Hh	+	˅arm [s] [may be M] (Be)	Hd
+	purse (Be)	Cg	–	arm [s] [may be M] (Be)	Hd
+	rabbits (Ro)	A	+	arm with thumb and index finger [may be M] (Lo)	Hd
–	rat (Be)	A	–	bird (Be)	A
–	rocks (Be)	Ls	+	branch, broken off (Mu)	Bt
+	sacks of gold (Be)	Mn	+	claws, crustacean's (Be)	Ad
+	˅shrubbery [may involve Y] (Be)	Bt	+	club (Bl)	Im
+	˅skull, ape's (Be)	An, Sc	+	feet (Ro)	Hd
+	skulls (Be)	An	+	fins, fish's (Bl)	Ad
+	sponge or something like that (Mu)	A?, Hh?	+	˅firewood (Be)	Bt
–	testicles (Be)	Hd, Sex	+	fish [es] (Be, Ga, Ro)	A
+	˅tree [s] [may involve Y] (Be)	Bt	+	fish, flying (Ro)	A
+	x-ray, stomach (Be)	An	+	foot, human (Be)	Hd
			+	foot, ostrich's (Be)	Ad
			+	foot, race horse's (Be)	Ad
			+	foot, rooster's (LU)	Ad
			–	hands [may be M] (Be)	Hd
			M+	˅hands, outstretched (Be)	Hd
			FY–	isles in water (Be)	Ls
			+	Italy (Be)	Ge

ATYPICAL
D 4 with D 5

	Response	Code
–	fly (Be)	A

D 4 with Dds 24 (scored Ds)

	Response	Code
FY+	landscape, winter (Be)	Ls

III — D 5 cont'd

+	leg, deer's (Be)	Ad	
+	^v leg [s], human (Be)	Hd	
-	Madagascar (Be)	Ge	
FV-	v mountains, two equally high (Lo)	Ls	
FV-	v peninsula, surrounded by water, white part is deep water [D 10 is low land because it is lighter shade] (Be)	Ls	
FY-	v reef (Be)	Ls	
-	seaweed (Be)	Bt	
+	skeleton, human, part of (Be)	An	
+	stick (Be)	Bt	
-	tree (Be)	Bt	
+	^v tree limb, branch (Be, Bo)	Bt	

+	head, bird's (Be)	Ad	
-	head, bug's (Be)	Ad	
+	head, chicken's (Be)	Ad	
+	head, dog's (Be)	Ad	
+	head, rooster's (Be)	Ad	
+	heads, monkeys' (Ro)	Ad	
+	heads, Negroes' (Ro)	Hd	
+	heads, skeletons' (Be)	An	
+	mask (Be)	Hd?, Rc?	
-	monkey (Be)	A	
+	rock (Be)	Ls	
-	shell, clam, broken (Be)	Ad	
FT	v shell, sea, round and slight markings in middle (Kl)	Na	

III - D 6

-	acorn (Be)	Bt	
FV-	bridge in Chinese rock garden (Be)	Ls, Ar	
-	coconut (Be)	Bt	
-	football [s] (Be)	Rc	

ATYPICAL
D 6 with Dds 24 and D 8 (scored Ds)

FV+	tree with precipice or ravine with water [D 6 is "bunched leaves:" D 8 light variations are ripples] (Be)	Ls, Bt	

+	barrel (Be)	Hh
-	bivalve (Be)	A
+	body, lower part (Be)	Hd
+	bones, pelvic (Be)	An
+	bowl (Be)	Hh
-	brain section, fourth (Be)	An, Sc
-	car, hand (Be)	Tr
+	cauldron, witches' (Be)	Hh, My
-	cord, spinal (Be)	An
-	crab (Be)	A
FY- ∨	creature, misshapen, dark, with huge protruding eyes (Bi)	Hd?, Ad?
FV+	entrance, park (Be)	Ls
-	eyeglasses (Be)	Im
+	fireplace (Be)	Ar
-	insect (Be)	A
+	jug (Be)	Hh
+	kettle (Be)	Hh
FY	landscape, moonlight, dark bush in foreground, lake reflecting moon in background (Kl)	Ls, Bt
-	lungs (Be)	An

-	mask (Be)	Hd?, Rc?
+	nest (Be)	Na
+	pail (Be)	Hh
FV+	painting, Japanese, of bluff (Be)	Art
+	pelvis (Be)	An
+	property, stage (Be)	Oj
+	sacroiliac (Be)	An
FY.V+ ∨	shrubbery, water, and shadows (Be)	Ls, Bt
-	spider (Be)	A
+	stove (Be)	Hh
+	tub (Be)	Hh
-	vertebra, cervical (Be)	An
-	womb (Be)	An, Sex

+	bones (Be)	An
-	brain-stem section (Be)	An, Sc
FY+	brook (Be)	Ls
+	chest (Be)	Hd
-	chest with ribs (Bo)	Hd, An?
FY-	clouds (Be)	Cl
YF	clouds after rain, beginning to clear up (Oe)	Cl
+	^v crab (Be)	A
-	Crucifixion (Be)	Rl
-	face (Be)	Hd
+	fireplace (Be)	Ar
+	firewood pieces (Be)	Bt
-	fountain (Be)	Ls
-	fox without tail (Lo)	A
FV+	v gate, Heaven's (Be)	Rl
-	genitalia, female (Be)	Hd, Sex
+	v goblet [with or without contained Dds] (Be)	Hh
-	jack-o'-lantern (Be)	Rc
FY+	lamp in fog (Be)	Cl
FY+	landscape with inlets (Be)	Ls
-	lungs (Be)	An
+	pelvis (Be)	An
+	precipice (Be)	Ls
+	pubis (Be)	Hd, Sex
+	pumpkin [with or without contained Dds] (Be)	Bt
FV.Y+	> reflection of land in swamp water (Be)	Ls
+	rib [s] (Be)	An
FY-	river (Be)	Ls
+	sacroiliac (Be)	An
+	shell, crab, frayed (Be)	Ad
+	skeleton (Be)	An
-	skeleton, part of (Bo)	An
+	sternum (Be)	An
-	thorax, part of (Mu)	An
F	v toffee being pulled apart (Kl)	Fd
+	trees (Vi)	Bt
-	vagina [with or without contained Dds] (Be)	An, Sex
+	v vase [with or without contained Dds] (Be)	Hh
+	vertebra (Vi)	An

III — D 8 cont'd

FY+	water, shore and creeks (Be)	Ls
+	wood, splintered (Be)	Bt

ATYPICAL
Dd projecting into D 8

-	stalactites (Be)	Mn, Na

III - D 9

M+	˅Africans with feet up (Be)	H
-	animal [s] (Be)	A
-	animal [s], with left leg lifted (Be)	A
+	bird (Be)	A
+	BOYS, COLORED [may be M] (Be)	H
+	CHARACTERS IN CARTOON [may be M] (Be)	H, Art
+	chicken [s] (Be)	A
-	clouds [may involve Y] (Be)	Cl
+	design on wall (Be)	Art
-	dogs (Be)	A
+	DOLL, ANIMATED [may be M] (Be)	H, Rc
+	duck (Be)	A
+	DUMMIES [may be M] (Be)	H
+	˅gentlemen, caricatured [may be M] (Be)	H, Art
-	lamb (Be)	A
+	MEN [may be M] (Be)	H
-	monkey [s] (Be)	A
M+	˅Negro [es], caricatured, in grotesque dress, kicking, praying, primitive (Be)	H, Art
+	ostrich [es] (Be)	A
+	PEOPLE [may be M] (Be)	H
+	scarecrow (Be)	H, Ru
-	sheep (Be)	A
FY+	˅swamp-land (Be)	Ls
-	turtle, mud (Be)	A

ATYPICAL
D 9 with Dds 23

+	map with arm reaching into sea and water (Be)	Ge

+ ˇfinger [s] [may be M] (Be) — Hd
- finger [s] [may be M] (Be) — Hd
+ ˇhand [s] [may be M] (Be) — Hd
- hand [s] [may be M] (Be, Bl) — Hd
M+ hand, pointing finger as abstract sign of warning (Kl) — Hd, Ab
+ hoof, cloven (Be) — Ad
+ hoof, cow's (Be) — Ad
+ hoof, deer's (Be) — Ad
+ hoof, horse's (Be) — Ad
+ hoof, lamb's (Be) — Ad
+ hoof, race horse's (Be) — Ad
+ hoof, satyr's (Be) — Ad, My
- paw (Be) — Ad
+ shoe, woman's; the heel, however, should be a little broader (Bo) — Cg
+ shoes, high heel (Be) — Cg
- woman (Be) — H

FV- animal, image of (Be) — A
- animal, skinned (Be) — A
- animals, unspecified (Ro) — A
- bird (Be) — A
+ ˇbird [s] (Be) — A
- bird, stuffed (Ro) — A
+ birds in men's clothing [may be M] (Be) — A, Cg
- bulb [s], plant (Be) — Bt
+ ˇcliffs, rocky [likely to be a V response] (Be) — Ls
- dog (Be) — A
FY- ˇdog, shaggy (Be) — A
+ Donald Duck [may be M] (Be) — A, H
+ ˇfigure, Ku Klux Klan [may be M] (Be) — H
- insects (Be) — A
FV+ man, image of (Be) — H
M- ˆman standing (Be) — H
+ ˇman, half, half dog (Be) — Hd, Ad
+ men [may be M] (Be) — H
M+ person standing with hand on hip, elbow sticking out (Kl) — H

III — D 11 cont'd

+	persons, two [may be M] (LU)	H
Y	photograph section in the sky (Be)	Art, Sc
-	rooster (Be)	A
-	roosters fighting (Be)	A
+	∨ seals, trick (Be)	A
+	skeleton (Be)	An
V	terrain, mountainous (Be)	Ls
-	thigh, woman's (Be)	Hd
+	torso, human (Be)	Hd
+	vase (LU)	Hh
+	women with legs missing (Be)	Hd

ATYPICAL
D 11 with D 4

TF-	messy substance or furry; it is dripping; it hangs (Be)	?
+	∨ tree, wind-blown, desert (Be)	Bt

+	∨ crab (Be)	A
+	∨ frog (Be)	A
M+	∨ human with arms up (Be)	H
+	∨ landscape [may involve V] (Be)	Ls
-	man [may be M] (Be)	H
+	park [may involve V] (Be)	Ls
+	pelvic cavity formation (Be)	An
FY+	scene, snow (Be)	Na

ATYPICAL
D 12 with D3

-	face (Be)	Hd
FY-	man with white collar and tie (Be)	H, Cg
CF-	miscarriage (Be)	An, Blood

D 12 with Dds 24

FY.FV+	forest and road (Be)	Ls, Bt

III - Dd 21

+	ˇbeaks, birds' [bird may be named] (Be)	Ad
-	head, cow's (Be)	Ad
-	head, deer's (Be)	Ad
-	head, fox's (Be)	Ad
-	˄ˇhead, mouse's (Be)	Ad
-	˄ˇhead, rat's (Be)	Ad
-	head, wolf's (Be)	Ad

III - Dd 22

+	ˇbird [s] (Be)	A
M-	dancer, ballet (Be)	H
+	ˇeagle in flight (Be)	A
+	˄˃eagle on branch (Be)	A, Bt
-	head, deer's (Be)	Ad
-	mountain (Be)	Ls
-	North America (Be)	Ge
-	saddle (Be)	Tr
+	˄turkey (Be)	A

III - Dds 23

+	design, border (Be)	Art
-	dress, woman's, of 19th Century (Be)	Cg
FV -	ˆeagle, flying (Be)	A
-	head, dog's (Be)	Ad
-	river (Bl)	Ls
-	sea (Bl)	Ls
+	sea, Adriatic (Be)	Ge
+	water (Be)	Ls

ATYPICAL
both Dds 23 as one

-	mushroom (Be)	Bt

III - Dds 24

FY.FV+	avenue, shady, in a park where, on the horizon, are two trees (Bo)	Ls, Bt	
+	bowl (Be)	Hh	
+	chalice (Be)	Rl	
−	face, cat's (Be)	Ad	
+	˅ flower, conventionalized (Be)	Bt, Art	
CF−	goblet with blood in it (Bo)	Hh, Blood	
+	lamp with glass chimney (Be)	Hh	
−	mountain with snow (Bo)	Ls	
+	˅ mushroom (Be)	Bt	
FV+	˅ road, country (Be)	Ls, Ru	
+	˅ shirt front (Be)	Cg	
M−	soldier, moving down (Be)	H	
+	snow (Be)	Na	
+	stencil (Be)	Im	
FV.FY+	street, dusty; it extends broadly into distance. There [D 4] two trees with full, overhanging foliage. The trees throw shadows on street. Far in background [D 8] one sees again a crippled tree with dry branches (Bi)	Ls, Bt	
?	waistcoat, crumpled, white (Oe)	Cg	

+	winter (LU)		Ab

III - Dd 25

FC+	˅ beak and comb, rooster's (Bl)		Ad
FC+	esophagus (Be)		An
+	pole (Be)		Im
+	queues, Chinese (Be)		Hd
+	rope (Be)		Im
+	stick (Be)		Im
+	string (Be)		Im
−	tail, bird's (Be)		Ad
−	tail, lion's (Be)		Ad
+	ureter [may be FC+] (Be)		An

III - Dd 26

+	erection (Be)	Hd, Sex
+	pants (Be)	Cg
+	penis (Be)	Hd, Sex
+	skirt (Be)	Cg

III - Dd 27

+	breast (Be)	Hd, Sex
-	cap, auto radiator (Be)	Art, Tr
+	dog in a wind-storm (Bo)	A
+	head, kitten's (Lo)	Ad
+	˅ head, rodent's (Be)	Ad
-	nose, dog's (Be)	Ad

III - Dd 28

-	bone (Be)	An
-	tooth (Be)	Hd

III - Dd 29

-	chicken (Be)	A
-	person (Be)	H

III - Dd 30

-	foot (Be)	Hd
+	hand [s] [may be M] (Be)	Hd
-	penis (Be)	Hd, Sex

W excluding D 2

-	basket (Be)	Hh
-	hat (Be)	Cg
+	vase (Be)	Hh

W excluding D 2 and D 3

+	figure, human [D 5 as arms; may be M] (Be)	H
+	monster [D 5 as arms; may be M] (Be)	H

upper half entire

-	letter W (Be)	Al

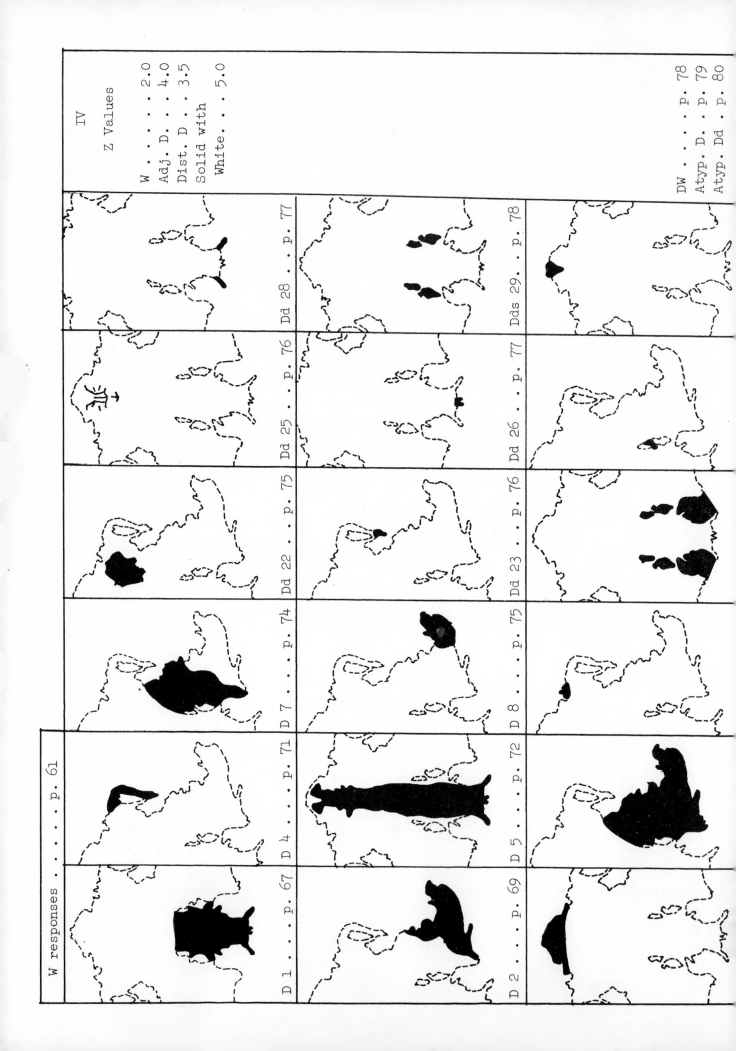

IV

Z Values

W 2.0
Adj. D . . . 4.0
Dist. D . . 3.5
Solid with
White . . . 5.0

DW . . . . . p. 78
Atyp. D. . . p. 79
Atyp. Dd . . p. 80

W responses . . . . . p. 61

D 1 . . . p. 67   D 4 . . . p. 71   D 7 . . . p. 74   Dd 22 . . p. 75   Dd 25 . . p. 76   Dd 28 . . p. 77

D 2 . . . p. 69   D 5 . . . p. 72   D 8 . . . p. 75   Dd 23 . . p. 76   Dd 26 . . p. 77   Dds 29 . . p. 78

+	adornment at top of piece of furniture (Ro)	Art, Hh
+	anchor (LU)	Tr
+	animal (Ga)	A
+	ANIMAL [any massive furred] (Be)	A
+	animal [any unusual form, e.g., prehistoric] (Be)	A
-	animal [lateral extensions are called the legs] (Ro)	A
+	animal from bottom of the sea [kind of cuttle-fish] (Ro)	A
+	animal, sea (Be)	A
+	animal, undefinable (Bl)	A
+	APE, HUGE (Be)	A
Y	atmosphere, thunder-storm (Bi)	Na
M+	BABOON, READY TO POUNCE (Be)	A
+	bat (Be)	A
+	bat (Ga, Ro)	A
+	bat hanging upside down (Be)	A
M+	bear, bowing (Ro)	A
M+	bear, dancing, without head (Bl)	Ad
M+	BEAR DOING CHARLESTON (Be)	A
+	BEARSKIN (Be)	A

-	bee (Be)	A
-	beetle (Be)	A
-	beetle [large lateral projections should be wings and middle part, the head. Thin lateral projections are legs] (Ob)	A
+	bell with tongue [lower middle part] (Bo)	Mu
-	bell-shaped (Be)	Mu
+	bird (Be)	A
+	block, rough design of (Be)	Oj
M+	BOY IN RACCOON COAT (Be)	H, A
-	brain section (Be)	An, Sc
-	bug (Be)	A
+	butterfly (Be)	A
+,	butterfly shape (Bo)	A
+	carcass, reindeer (Be)	A
+	carpet (Be)	Hh
FY-	castle, a god's, of black basalt, high up on sky-tail rocks (Bi)	Ar, My
FV+	cave, outside of, the white representing the inside [with Dds 24 and 29, i.e., Ws] (Be)	Ls
+	chandelier (Be)	Hh

IV — W cont'd

YF	cinders (Bi)	Mn
FY+	cloudiness (Be)	Cl
+	clouds [may involve Y] (Be)	Cl
YF	clouds, torn, very dark (Bi)	Cl
+	clown (Be)	H
FY+	coat, completely torn — such old rags. There ["snakes"] the rest of the sleeves (Bi)	Cg
-	coat-of-arms (Ro, Bo)	Art
FY+	coat-of-arms on funeral banner (Bi)	Art, Dh
M+	COLLEGIATE IN BEARSKIN COAT GOING TO FOOTBALL GAME (Be)	H, A
Y	colors, two, now lighter, now darker; on both sides the same pretty impression (Ro)	Ab
+	column with winged figures (Be)	Ar, Art
-	coral, broken (Be)	A
FY	covering, velvet, impression of (Mu)	Hh
-	crab (Be)	A
+	creature, mythological (Be)	A, My
+	crest [i.e., official seal] (Be)	Art
YF	crystal-like something (Bi)	Mn
Y	darkness, because it is black (Be)	Ab
+	design (Be)	Art
-	devil, reminds one of a picture (Bl)	H, Art
M.FY+	devil squatting as if he were going to start out in next moment (Bi)	H, Rl
+	drawing by baby (Be)	Art
M+	dwarfs, two, leaning on tree trunk, with dunce caps [upper lateral projection] and potato bellies (Mu)	H, Bt
-	eagle (Be)	A
-	elephant (Be)	A
+	elephants, two, back to back (Be)	A
+	embryo (Be)	An, Sc
+	escutcheon (Be)	Art
+	falcon, flying (Ro)	A
+	fern (Be)	Bt
+	figure, dream, in an anxiety dream, poisonous (Bo)	H, Ab
+	figure, gloomy [probably involves Y] (Be)	H, Ab
M+	figure on chair (Ro)	H, Hh

+	figure on fountain (Ro)	H, Ls
M+	figure, sitting (Ro)	H
M	figure, slender, very small, seen from back, turning away (Bi)	H
-	fish (Be)	A
+	fish (Ga)	A
-	flea (Ro)	A
+	flower (Be)	Bt
-	fly, magnified (Be)	A
FV+	forest, reflected in lake (Be)	Bt, Ls
+	fossil, animal (Be)	A, Sc
+	fountain, Indian elephant; above the basin, below the pedestal (Ro)	A, Ls
+	frieze bands (Ro)	Art
+	FUR, FOX (Be)	A
+	Gambrinus on an inn sign (Ro)	H, Art
+	giant (Be)	H, My
M.FY+	giant, gruesome, seen from below [feet are enormously large and the head small] (Bi)	H, My
M+	giants, two sleeping, allegorical representation of, with caps hanging down (Bl)	H, My

A	GORILLA, READY TO POUNCE (Be)	M+
Im	governor on engine (Be)	-
Ad	head, ant's (Be)	-
Ad	head, buffalo's (Be)	+
Ad	head, dog's (Be)	-
Ad	head, fat animal's [lateral projections are ears; middle piece is snout] (Ob)	+
Ad	head, ram's (Be)	+
An	heart, degenerated (Ro)	-
A	HIDE (Be, Vr)	+
A	hide, animal's (Ro)	+
A	horse (Be)	-
Ab	impressions, sinister (Be)	+
Hh	incense burner (Be)	+
A	insect (Ga)	+
Art	insignia (Be)	+
Ab	integration (Be)	+
A	jellyfish (Be)	+
A	kangaroo [because in middle of black space there are some heads visible, and the kangaroo has such a belly-pouch] (Ro)	-

	kernel, walnut (Be)	Bt
+	><landscape, any, and reflection (Be)	Ls
+	leaf, partly decayed (Be)	Bt
+	lv̌yre (Be)	Mu
M.Y	Madonna with spread-out arms hovering above the clouds (Bi)	H, Rl
+	man, bushman (Be)	H, Ay
M.FV+	m̂an [D 2] on sleigh [D 6] riding with ice reflected below (Be)	H, Tr
M-	man, gigantic, with mighty feet is sitting here (Ro)	H
M+	MAN IN BEARSKIN COAT, WALKING AWAY, HEAD BURIED IN COLLAR, FLAPPING HIS ARMS (Be)	H, A
M+	man walking (Be)	H
+	man with head cut off (Be)	Hd
FY+	map of an island with rugged coast (Bi)	Ge
FY+	map with surrounding water on each side [scored Ws] (Be)	Ge
+	mollusc (Be)	A
M+	monster, coming at you (Be)	A
+	monster [may be M] (Ro)	A, My
+	MONSTER IN SHEEP SKIN, WITH LARGE BOOTS [may be M] (Ro)	H, -Cg
M+	Moritz [of Busch's "Max and Moritz," when he fell into the dough (Ro)	H
+	moth (Be)	A
FY+	Niagara Falls [with D 6 as mountains, D 5 as the water, and Dds 29 and Dds 24 as tunnel. All elements of this original content are +, hence the response is +; scored Ws] (Be)	Ls
Y	nightmare (Bi)	Ab
+	object, mashed (Be)	Oj
+	overcoat (Be)	Cg
+	pattern in art (Be)	Art
+	PELT (Be, Ob, Vr)	A
-	pelvis (Be)	An
M+	phantom, dancing (Be)	H
M+	piano player who is violently banging on his piano [upper lateral projections seen as arms, lower lateral projections as legs enlarged in perspective and grotesquely] (Mu)	H, Mu
Y	pictures, night, lots of (Bi)	Ab
Y	picture, peculiar, black, grayish (Ro)	Art

Y	picture, symbolic, wonderful [on top a small dominion, so dreamy, so gentle, like my childhood. And this nobility is surrounded by night, so animal-like, and from below springs up the breath of the devil] (Bi)	Art, Ab
−	plant (Be)	Bt
+	plant, some kind of, or something like that (Ro)	Bt
+	polyp (Ro)	A
FV+	pond in woods with distant landscape reflected (Be)	Ls, Bt
FV+	>reflection in lake (Be)	Ls
+	ROBE, FUR (Be)	A
+	root which has been dug out (Mu)	Bt
+	rug, any (Be)	Hh
+	rug, fancy (Ro)	Hh
+	RUG, FUR (Be)	A
+	sacrum (Be)	An
FY+	scarecrow, draped with dark cloth (Bi)	H, Ru
−	seaweed (Be)	Bt
+	⌄SKIN (Be)	A
+	^⌄SKIN, ANIMAL'S (Be, Vr, Ga)	A

TF+	SKIN, ANIMAL'S, VERY WARM, OR COOL: COOL BECAUSE IT IS DARK; WOULD FEEL WARM IF AROUND A PERSON (Be)	A
+	⌄SKIN, LION'S (Be)	A
+	SKIN, TIGER'S (Be)	A
+	sloth (Be)	A
+	⌄sloth (Bl)	A
FY+	smoke, column of, springing up sharply in the middle and dividing and spreading, to lose itself within at the top [the black-and-white and the form together determine the interpretation] (Ro)	Fi
FY+	smoke from an exploding mine (Bo)	Fi
YF	smoke clouds, which burst up from there and then drag along the country [points to the side projections]. Like smoke banners in the rain (Bi)	Fi
Y	smoke, because it is black (Be)	Fi
Y+	smoke, clouds of, from explosion (Be)	Fi
−	⌄snowflake (Be)	Na
M+	⌄somebody sitting on stump (Ro)	H, Bt
−	spider (Be)	A
−	sponge (Be)	A

IV — W cont'd

+	squid (<u>Be</u>)	A
+	starfish, developmental form of (<u>Be</u>)	A, Sc
+	statue (<u>Be</u>)	Art
+	structure, oriental (<u>Be</u>)	Ar
+	student, Harvard (<u>Be</u>)	H
+	temple, Chinese (<u>Be</u>)	Ar, Rl
+	thistle (<u>Be</u>)	Bt
-	tick (<u>Be</u>)	A
+	v̂ tree (<u>Be</u>)	Bt
+	troll (<u>Be</u>)	H, My
FY+	underbrush, the lighter part is fern, the rest is forest (<u>Be</u>)	Bt
YF	underworld, tumult of black smoke and white bodies. One could say Dante's Inferno (<u>Bi</u>)	Ab, Fi
+	urn (<u>Be</u>)	Hh
+	vampire (<u>Bo</u>)	A
+	vertebrae (<u>Ga</u>)	An
+	wine-skin (<u>Be</u>)	Hh
M+	woman, knitting sitting (<u>Ro</u>)	H
-	womb, because there are two little heads inside (<u>Ro</u>)	An, Sex
YF	x-ray, animal (<u>Bi</u>)	An
YF	x-ray, half-decayed bones (<u>Bi</u>)	An
+	x-ray, man's body [may involve Y] (<u>Be</u>)	An
FY+	x-ray picture because of the shadings (<u>Mu</u>)	An
+	x-ray plate [may involve Y] (<u>Be</u>)	An

+	animal [s] (Be)	A
+	animals, most horned (Be)	A
+	BEETLE (Bo)	A
+	body, butterfly's, part of (Ro)	Ad
+	bug (Be)	A
+	ˇcastle (Be)	Ar
-	cat (Be)	A
+	caterpillar (Be)	A
+	coccyx (Be)	An
+	cord, spinal (Ga)	An
+	cow (Be)	A
+	ˇcrab, hermit (Be)	A
-	crayfish (Be)	A
+	ˇcrown, chess king's (Be)	Art, Rc
-	dog (Be)	A
-	eskimo (Ro)	H
—	face, alligator's (Be)	Ad
-	face, crocodile's (Be)	Ad
+	ˇfigure, Hindu (Be)	H
-	fountain (Be)	Ls
+	fur, piece of [may involve Y] (Be)	Ad

+	ˇghost (Be)	H
+	goat (Be)	A
-	head, alligator's (Be)	Ad
FY+	ˇhead, black animal's, which looks angry (Bi)	Ad, Ab
+	head, boar's (Be)	Ad
+	head, buffalo's (Be)	Ad
+	head, bull's (Be)	Ad
+	head, cow's (Be)	Ad
-	head, crocodile's (Be)	Ad
+	head, deer's (Be)	Ad
-	head, dog's (Be)	Ad
+	head, dragon's (Be)	Ad, My
-	head, fish's (Be)	Ad
+	head, fly's (Be)	Ad
-	head, horse's (Be)	Ad
+	ˇhead, human [frequently specific, e.g., king, head-hunter] (Be)	Hd
+	head, insect's (Be)	Ad
+	head, ox's (Bo)	Ad
-	head, rat's (Be)	Ad
-	head, rhinoceros' (Be)	Ad

67

IV — D 1 cont'd

+	head, snake's (Bo)	Ad
-	head, wolf's (Be)	Ad
+	heads, animals', most horned (Be)	Ad
+	heart, celery (Be)	Bt
+	hydra (Be)	A
+	idol (Be)	R1
-	insect (Be)	A
+	lamp (Be)	Hh
+	ˇlighthouse (Be)	Ar, Ls
+	medulla (Be)	An, Sc
+	ˇowl (Be)	A
+	owl (Ro)	A
+	pelt [may involve Y] (Be)	A
-	person (Be)	H
-	sea-horse (Be)	A
+	seat (Be)	Hh
Y+	smoke (Be)	Fi
-	snail (Be)	A
+	spine, section of (Be)	An, Sc
+	stool, piano (Mu)	Mu, Hh
+	stump (Be)	Bt

+	tail (Be)	Ad
+	tail, insect's (Ro)	Ad
+	totem pole (Be)	Ay
+	ˇtower, chess (Ro)	Ar, Rc
FV+	ˇtower, the front of a church, a steeple up at the top (Be)	Ar, Rl
+	tree trunk (Be)	Bt
+	urn with legs (Be)	Hh
+	vase (Be)	Hh
+	ˇvase, which becomes thinner at the top (Vi)	Hh
+	vertebra, spinal (Be)	An

ATYPICAL
D 1 with adjacent Dds

+	mouth, cave [may involve V] (Be)	Ls
FV+	tunnels made by ice [scored Ds] (Be)	Na

D 1, lower end Dd

+	ˇcrown (Be)	Art
+	ˇskull, prehistoric, with horns (Be)	An, Sc

IV -- D 1 cont'd

ATYPICAL
dot Dd in lower end

+	eyes, any animal's [score + for "eyes" even when D 1 as "animal" named, e.g., fish, would be -] (Be)	Ad

IV - D.2

+	bear (Be)	A
+	bird (Be)	A
-	boat (Be)	Tr
-	branch [es] (Be)	Bt
+	Cape Cod (Be)	Ge
+	cloud [s] [may involve Y] (Be)	Cl
YF+	clouds, dark (Be)	Cl
-	cow (Be)	A
+	dog [usually, but not necessarily, > or <] (Be)	A
+	dog, any named breed [usually, but not necessarily >or<] (Be)	A
-	˅ elk (Be)	A
+	emblem (Be)	Art

+	face (Be)	Hd
+	feet, human (Be)	Hd
-	grass (Be)	Bt
+	head (Be)	Hd
-	head, lamb's (Be)	Ad
-	head, seal's (Be)	Ad
M+	∧>< human [figure is usually woman, may be man, nearly always old or bowed] (Be)	H
-	˅ jaw, moose's (Be)	Ad
+	leg, animal's (Be)	Ad
M+	man reading book (Be)	H
+	map (Be)	Ge
-	neck and head, turkey's (Be)	Ad
-	˅ Norway (Be)	Ge
+	peninsula (Be)	Ge
M+	∧ person, old, praying (Be)	H, Rl
-	pig (Be)	A
-	profile, moose's (Be)	Ad
+	shoe (Be)	Cg
YF+	smoke (Be)	Fi
+	totem pole (Be)	Ay

IV – D 2 cont'd

+		wing, bat's (Be)	Ad
+		>woman, ugly old [may be M] (Be)	H

ATYPICAL
Dd projecting from lower median edge of D 2 (scored Dd)

F		pincers, two, spider's (Lo)	Ad
FY		plasticine, formed by awkward children's hands (Bo)	Rc
+		>poplar (Ro)	Bt

IV - D 3

-		anus (Be)	Hd, Anal
+	^∨>< butterfly (Be)		A
-		candle (Be)	Hh
+		castle, Chinese (Bl)	Ar
+		collar, lace (Be)	Cg, Pr
+		cross section through flower cup and leaves (Bo)	Bt, Sc
+		delta (Be)	Ge?, Ls?
+		fan (Be)	Pr
+		flower (Be, Ga, LU)	Bt
+		gryphon seen from front (Ro)	A, My
+		head [usually odd, e.g., of mythical human or strange animal] (Be)	Hd?, Ad?
+		head, cat's (Be)	Ad
-		head, cabbage (Be)	Bt
FY		head, human (LU)	Hd
-		head, walrus' (Be)	Ad
+		impression, pleasant, of beautiful ornaments (Bl)	Art, Ab
+		insignia, air corps (Be)	Art
+		lichen (Be)	Bt
-		scuttle-fish (Be)	A
+		secretion, squid's (Be)	Oj
-		shell, sea (Be)	Na
-		skin, animal's (Be)	A
-		squid (Be)	A
+		vagina (Be)	An, Sex
-		whiskers, cat's (Be)	Ad
+		wings, insect's [may be FV if transparency is indicated] (Be)	Ad

−	alligator [s] (Be)	A
−	animal (Be)	A
+	animals (Bl)	A
+	animal with long neck (Be)	A
+	aorta (Be)	An
+	arms, swimmer's (Be)	Hd
−	belt (Be)	Cg
−	bill, pelican's (Be)	Ad
−	bird (Be)	A
+	bone, hip (Vi)	An
+	branch, tree (Be)	Bt
+	branch, weeping willow (Be)	Bt
+	branches, two gnarled (Ro)	Bt
+	cap, stocking (Be)	Cg
−	cat (Be)	A
+	caterpillars (Ro)	A
+	ˇclaws, crab's (Be)	Ad
+	ˇclaws, lobster's (Be)	Ad
−	ears, dog's (Be)	Ad
−	ears, elephant's (Be)	Ad
+	elephant, something from (Ro)	Ad

+	figure, human [may be M] (Be)	H
−	flippers, seal's (Be)	Ad
FT−	grease, dirty, dripping (Be)	Oj
+	handles (Be)	Im
+	hands (Be)	Hd
−	harpoon (Be)	Im
+	head, bird's [any bird with prominent neck] (Be)	Ad
+	head, eagle's (Be)	Ad
+	head, goose's (Be)	Ad
+	head, turkey's (Be)	Ad
−	hook (Be)	Im
+	hooks (LU)	Im
+	horn, animal's (Be)	Ad
+	horn, bull's (Be)	Ad
+	horn, goat's (Be)	Ad
−	horse (Be)	A
+	icicle (Be)	Na
−	legs, human (Be)	Hd
+	lizard (Be)	A
+	neck, goose's (Be)	Ad

–	oar-locks (Be)	Im
+	snake [s] (Be, Ro)	A
+	sucker (Mu)	Bt
+	tree (Be)	Bt
+	∨ tree roots, fantastic (Be)	Bt
+	trunk and tusk, elephant's (Be)	Ad
+	weasel (Ro)	A
M+	witches, two, who are dancing and showing something (B1)	H, My

ATYPICAL
D 4 with Dd 21

+	angel, black [may be M] (Be)	H, R1
–	cat (Be)	A
+	human, any [may be M] (Be)	H
M+	woman, dancing (Be)	H
M+	worshiper (Be)	H, Rl

D 4 with adjacent Dd

+	head, elephant's (Be)	Ad

–	backbone (Ro)	An
+	column (Be)	Ar
+	column, spinal (Be)	An
FV+	crater, volcano (Be)	Ls
+	∨ devil, little [may be M] (Be)	H, Rl
FY+	∨ figure, gruesome [only legs and abdomen are clear; on top it looks as if it were wrapped in a cloud] (Bi)	H, Cl
FY+	figure, veiled with a black cloth	H, Cg
–	fish (Be)	A
+	∨ fountain (Be)	Ls
–	fur [may involve Y] (Be)	A
–	insect (Be)	A
+	lady [may be M] (Be)	H
+	man [may be M] (Be)	H
+	∨ man, of whom one can see well only legs and hip region; whereas the upper part of body [dark region in middle column] in unclear (Bi)	H
–	Meyer life chart (Be)	Oj
+	neural groove (Be)	An, Sc
–	organs, female sex (Be)	Hd, Sex

IV -- D 5 cont'd

+	penis, dissection of (Be)	Hd, Sex
+	plant, big (Lo)	Bt
+	post (Be)	Oj
+	river (Be)	Ls
FV+	ski slide marked out of path on side of hill (Be)	Ls
+	statue (Be)	Art
-	street over a mountain (Lo)	Ge (according to orig- inal author)
+	totem pole (Be)	Ay
-	tree, fir (Be)	Bt
+	tree trunk (Be)	Bt
+	x-ray [may involve Y] (Be)	An

ATYPICAL
D 5, upper half

+	∨ human in art (Be)	H, Art
-	legs, woman's (Be)	Hd
+	person, deformed (Be)	H
+	x-ray, spinal column [may involve Y] (Be)	An

IV - D 6

+	boots, giant's, seven-league pair [may be M] (Be)	Cg, My
FY+	clouds, thunder (Bo)	Cl
+	feet, two, big, in rough boots [may be M] (Be)	Hd, Cg
-	fort (Be)	Ar
+	Italy (Be)	Ge
+	legs [may be M] (Be)	Hd
+	shoe (Be)	Cg
+	shoes, worn out (Ro)	Cg
FY+	smoke from volcano (Be)	Fi, Ls
FY+	sky, stormy (Be)	Na
+	trousers with feet in them (Be)	Hd, Cg
+	∨ wings, bat's (Be)	Ad
M+	∧ woman, stooped over, who has to carry a load (Bi)	H

+	Africa (Be)	Ge
+	animal [s], formalized, as on coat-of-arms (Be)	A, Art
+	arabesque (Be)	Art
+	∨ arch of trees [both D 7 as one D] (Be)	Bt
-	bird (Be)	A
M+	∨ brownies, two, facing each other (Mu)	H, My
+	∨ chicken (Be)	A
M+	∨ children, two, facing each other (Mu)	H
+	∨ crags (Be)	Ls
-	∨ elephant (Be)	A
+	∨ figure human (Be)	H
-	^>< figure, human [may be M] (Be)	H
+	∨ figure, male [may be M] (Be)	H
-	flowers, fantastic, with tube-shaped chalice (Bi)	Bt, Art
FY+	∨ ghosts, two, upper part of bodies of, with dunce caps (Bi)	Hd, Cg
-	handles, jar (Be)	Im, Hh
+	∨ ladies, Spanish [may be M] (Be)	H
+	∨ monk [may be M] (Ro)	H, Rl
-	∨ mouse (Be)	A
+	∨ nuns [may be M] (Be)	H, Rl
M.FY	∨ nuns in black robes praying (Kl)	H, Rl
+	queens, two [may be M] (Be)	H
+	∨ rocks (Be)	Ls
+	∨ rooster (Be)	A
-	roots (Be)	Bt
+	∨ satyr (Ro)	H, My
+	seal (Be)	A
+	^∨ sea-lion (Be)	A
+	South America (Be)	Ge
+	statue (Be)	Art
+	tapir (Be)	A
-	tree [s] (Be)	Bt
+	^ weasel or similar kind of animal (Bi)	A
M+	∨ women in sunbonnets, looking at each other (Be)	H, Cg

ATYPICAL
D 7 with adjacent Dd

+	animal (Be)	A
+	water from fountain (Be)	Ls

+	^v face (Be)	Hd
+	> face, clown's (Ro)	Hd
+	> face, little, with long nose (Bl)	Hd
+	gnome [may be M] (Be)	H, My
+	head, man's (Be)	Hd
+	heads, grotesque (Be)	Hd
FV+	landscape, distant (Be)	Ls
-	squirrel (Be)	A

IV – Dd 22

+	face, girl's (Be)	Hd
+	face, woman's (Be)	Hd
+	head, dog's (Be)	Ad
+	man (Be)	H
+	profile (Be)	Hd
+	teeth, animal's (Be)	Ad

ATYPICAL
Dd 22, both, with interspace

-	butterfly (Be)	A

IV – D 8

-	bird (Ro)	A
+	camel (Be)	A
-	crocodile (Ro)	A
+	dwarfs [may be M] (Du)	H, My
+	face (Be)	Hd
-	fishes (Ro)	A
-	> Florida (Be)	Ge
+	form, human (Be)	H
+	gargoyle (LU)	Art
+	head, animal's (Be)	Ad
+	head, pig's (Be)	Ad
+	head with Colonial wig (Be)	Hd, Pr
+	^v heads, dogs' (Ro)	Ad
+	man, old, of the mountain (Be)	H
+	seals (Ro)	A
+	wings, two (Ro)	Ad
M+	> woman bent over book (Ro)	H
M+	woman, bent over, old, standing before a tombstone (Ro)	H, Dh
+	> woman with bundle of wood on her back [no movement seen] (Ro)	H, Bt

IV - Dd 23

+	head, bird's (Be)	Ad

IV - Dds 24

+	bird (Be)	A
+	duck (Be)	A
+	fretwork cuttings (Ro)	Art
+	head, dog's (Be)	Ad
+	ponds or little lakes on a mountain (Lo)	Ls
FY+	street, empty — if one would imagine having to walk through its narrow passage and then suddenly a monster [middle column] would block one's way (Bi)	Ls, A

ATYPICAL
Dds 24 and Dds 29

+	arch (Be)	Ar
+	coves and inlets (Be)	Ls
+	lakes (Be)	Ls
+	moth holes in a rug (Be)	Hh
FV+	tunnels (Be)	Ls

IV - Dd 25

+	face, animal's (Be)	Ad
+	face, human, any (Be)	Hd
+	head, bear's (Be)	Ad
+	head, cat's (Be)	Ad
+	head, dog's (Be)	Ad
+	head, lion's (Be)	Ad
+	head, monkey's (Be)	Ad

IV - Dd 26

-	claw (Be)	Ad
-	clitoris (Be)	Hd, Sex
M	dancer, just her legs (Be)	Hd
-	hands (Be)	Hd
+	legs, human, with feet [may be M] (Be)	Hd
-	mouth (Be)	Hd
M	˅ supplication, feeling of (Be)	Hd, Ab
+	udder, cow's (Be)	Ad

ATYPICAL
Dd 26 and Dd 28

-	fingers (Be)	Hd
+	insect processes (Be)	Ad

IV - Dd 27

+	foot, animal's (Be)	Ad
-	foot, human (Be)	Hd
+	hoof, horse's (Be)	Ad

ATYPICAL
Dd 27 and dark area against

M+	˅ figures, two, little, who are resting their hands on some-thing (Ro)	H
M+	˅ man deliberately speculating about his money interests (Ro)	H

IV - Dd 28

-	leg [s], animal's (Be)	Ad
-	tusks (Be)	Ad

IV - Dds 29

+	swans (Ro)	A
M+	Virgin, praying (Ro)	H, Rl

IV - Dd 30

-	anus (Be)	Hd, Anal
-	apple core (Be)	Bt
+	crown, little (Ro)	Art
+	head, fox's (Bo)	Ad
-	heart (Be)	An
+	lips (Be)	Hd
-	thalamus (Be)	An, Sc
+	vagina (Be)	An, Sex
FY	vagina (Kl)	An, Sex

IV - DW

D 4

-	elephant (Be)	A
-	lobster (Be)	A

D 5

-	human intercourse (Be)	H, Sex

IV - ATYPICAL D

upper half entire

+	animal (Be)	A
+	butterfly (Be)	A
+	cord, spinal, section with nerves (Be)	An, Sc
+	cow with horns (Be)	A
+	head, animal's (Be)	Ad
+	head, ram's (Be)	Ad
+	skull, steer's (Be)	An

upper half entire, excluding D 3

+	embryo design (Be)	An, Sc
−	head, man's (Be)	Hd
−	reindeer (Be)	A
+	x-ray [may involve Y] (Be)	An

lower half entire

−	ˇanimal (Be)	A
+	ˇbat with wings (Be)	A
−	ˇbird, summer (Ro)	A
−	bone, pelvic (Be)	An

+	ˇcastle between two crags (Be)	Ar, Ls
M.FY+	ˇfigure, strange, with big head, gruesome eyes, and horns like a faun. Left and right are two nuns in black clothing; they are, of course, frightened by the head in the middle and yet they are rushing toward him. One can see by the waving scarves how they run toward him (Bi)	H, Rl
−	ˇfly, big (Be)	A
+	ˇfountain with seals on side (Be)	Ls, A
M+	ˇking, little, fairy tale, who is greeting two queens who are hurrying up from left and right (Ro)	H, My
M.FY	king, wandering through the dark halls of his palace because the night is the only time he can be by himself (Kl)	H, Ar
Y	rock design (Kl)	Ls
+	tail and two feet of animal (Be)	Ad
M+	ˇwomen, two, with floating scarves dancing around fountain [middle part] (Ro)	H, Ls

IV – ATYPICAL D cont'd

<u>entire lateral portion, excluding D 5</u>

FY- bushes and trees (<u>Bi</u>) ...... Bt

FY.M jungle scene, giant tree on the left, snarling snake on the right, left from center a frightened human being hiding behind a boulder (<u>Kl</u>) ...... A, H

YF rocks, like one sees in Bocklin's picture of the Death Island (<u>Bi</u>) ...... Ls

+ [>] swan swimming along the shore (<u>Ro</u>) ...... A, Ls

<u>W, excluding D 1</u>

+ bat (<u>Be</u>) ...... A

+ [∨]coat sleeves, back ripped out (<u>Be</u>) ...... Cg

+ gorilla (<u>Be</u>) ...... A

<u>W, excluding D 1 and D 2</u>

+ fur (<u>Be</u>) ...... A

+ rug, bearskin (<u>Be</u>) ...... A, Hh

<u>W, excluding D 1, D 2, and D 4</u>

+ skin, animal (<u>Be</u>) ...... A

<u>W, excluding D 1 and D 4</u>

+ gorilla (<u>Be</u>) ...... A

+ man, lower part of (<u>Be</u>) ...... Hd

<u>W, excluding D 4</u>

+ bat (<u>Be</u>) ...... A

+ skin, any animal's (<u>Be</u>) ...... A

IV - ATYPICAL Dd

<u>Dds between D 4 and main blot figure</u>

- head, Santa Claus' (<u>Be</u>) ...... Hd, My

V

Z Values

W 1.0
Adj. D 2.5
Dist. D 5.0
Solid with
White 4.0

DW . . . . . . p. 96
Atyp. D . . . . . p. 97

Dd 26 . .p. 95   Dds 27 . .p. 95   Dds 28 . .p. 95   Dds 29 . p. 95   Dd 30 . p. 95

Dds 28 may be included

Dds 27 may be included

Dds 29 may be included

D 8 . . p. 92   Dd 24 . .p. 95

D 9 . . p. 92   Dd 25 . . p. 94

Dd 23 . . p. 94

D 11 . . p. 93

D 10 . . p. 93

.D 10 . may be excluded

Horns may be excluded

D 4 . . . p. 87

D 5 . . p. 89

D 7 . . . p. 91

D 6 . . . p. 90

D 1 . . p. 85

D 2 . . p. 86

D 3 . . . p. 87

Note: Passive M is often evoked here. Figures may be seen lying, sitting, etc.

+	airplane (Be)	Tr
+	animal, flying (Ro)	A
+	animal, squashed (Be)	A
+	animal with plumes (Be)	A
-	animal with split back (Be)	A
-	animals, run into each other (Be)	A
-	animals, winged (Ro)	A
-	banana (Bo)	Bt
+	∧∨>< BAT (Be)	A
+	BAT (Ga, Ob, Vr)	A
+	bat (Ro)	A
+	bee (Be)	A
-	beetle (Be)	A
+	∧∨>< bird (Be)	A
+	bird (Ga, Ro)	A
-	body, human, part of (Be)	Hd
+	body, symmetrical, in a flying position, with two feelers (Ro)	A

-	bones, neck vertebra (Du)	An
-	bone structure, piece of hind part (Ro)	An
+	book ends, pair (Be)	Hh
+	bridge (Be)	Ar
+	bug (Be)	A
-	bulls, two, in fight (Be)	A
+	∧∨ BUTTERFLY (Be, Ga, Ob, Vr)	A
+	butterfly (Ro)	A
FY+	butterfly, dark (Bi)	A
FT+	cape, fur (Be)	Cg, Pr
-	chart, nautical (Be)	Tr
+	child in masquerade costume [may be M] (Be)	H, Cg
M+	Chinamen, two, who fell to death [the "ears of the bat" are the stiff arms of the Chinamen; the "legs of the bat" are lying pigtails; the "wings" are the smashed legs of the Chinamen] (Ro)	H, Dh
YF+	cloth, black, piece of (Be)	Oj
YF	cloud, which hangs in the sky (Bi)	Cl, Na
	cross section, half, nervous system (Be)	An, Sc

+	ˇcrow (Be)	A
M+	dancer [extravaganza] (Be)	H
Y	ˇdarkness (Be)	Ab
-	decoration (LU)	Art
-	deer, split (Be)	A
M+	devil flying, holding wide skirt (Be)	H, Cg
M.FY+	devil standing there in the middle covering with his bat wings two prostrate, dead women; it is as if the women were clad in a dark veil (Bi)	H, Dh
+	dog, flying (Mu)	A
-	drawing, geographical, of reservoir with two side inlets (Bo)	Ge
+	eagle (Be)	A
-	felt [may involve T] (Be)	Oj
M+	figures, human, sleeping back to back (Be)	H
-	fly (Be)	A
-	forests and rocks with windmill [upper medial] (Bl)	Ls, Ar
-	fowl in old dinging room picture (Be)	A, Art
-	fungus (Be)	Bt

FY.FT+	fur piece, torn (Be)	Cg
+	ghost, night [probably involves Y] (Bl)	H, Ab
-	grasshopper (Be)	A
-	ˇhead, cow's, with horns (Be)	Ad
+	hide [may involve T] (Be)	A
+	hill with trees at shore line (Be)	Ls, Bt
-	horsefly rocker [insect] (Be)	A
Y-	ink, widely smeared (Du)	Oj
+	insect (Vr)	A
+	insect, flattened (Be)	A
+	insect, spread out (Be)	A
+	insect, winged (Be)	A
-	island (LU)	Ls
+	kite, paper (Bo)	Rc
-	lake (Be)	Ls
+	land in water [probably involves Y] (Be)	Ls
+	landscape [when aerial is scored FV] (Be)	Ls
-	leaf, oak, part of (Be)	Bt
-	leaves, two, pressed (Be)	Bt

-	map [when aerial is scored FV] (Be)	Ge
-	map of United States (Be)	Ge
M+	men sleeping back to back (Be)	H
M+	men, two, in hammocks (Be)	H
M+	men, two, lying on benches (Be)	H
M.TF	men, two, reclining against tent made of black furry skins (Kl)	H
M+	Mephistopheles with cape (Be)	H, Cg
+	monster of prehistoric times [may involve Y] (Bi)	A
-	mops, two (Be)	Hh
-	mosquito (Be)	A
+	MOTH (Be)	A
+	moth (Ga, Ro)	A
YF	mountain slope darkly covered with woods (Bi)	Ls, Bt
-	openwork for clothing (Be)	Cg
-	owl (Be)	A
+	peacock design (Be)	A, Art
+	peacocks, two (Be)	A
+	plane, amphibian, form of earlier (Bo)	Tr

-	pond (Be)	Ls
+	rabbit, flying (Ro)	A
+	rabbit, with blanket stretched (Be)	A, Hh
+	rabbit monster with only one head and two bodies (Bo)	A
-	rams bucking each other (Be)	A
-	rug, animal [may involve T] (Ro)	A, Hh
M+	Satan with flowing robes (Be)	H, Cg
-	shoulder blades (Bl)	An
+	skin, animal [may involve T] (Be)	A
-	skins, two animal, laid together [may involve T] (Be)	A
YF-	smoke reflected in water (Be)	Fi, Ls
-	something split [unspecified] (Du)	Oj
+	squirrel, flying (Vr)	A
+	standard of Roman legions (Be)	Art, Ay
-	substantia nigra, section of (Be)	An, Sc
-	tent (Be)	Oj
-	Thuner lake [on account of its form] (Bo)	Ls
M+	vaudeville act — three people on a wire (Be)	H, Rc

Det.	Response	Content
–	wasp (Be)	A
M+	∧> woman — the thighs ["bat's wings"] broadly extended; in the middle, the sex organ; one can look into it; in the back ["bat's ears"] like clasped hands (Bi)	H, Sex
M–	⌄> woman dancing (Be)	H
M+	woman dancing, with cape (Be)	H, Cg
M.FY+	∧> woman in black veil, with arms stretched high, falling backwards (Bi)	H, Cg
M+	∧> woman, old, carrying two umbrellas under her arm (Ro)	H, Im
M+	women sleeping back to back (Be)	H
–	wolves, running, meeting (Be)	A
–	x-ray, nervous system section (Be)	An

FQ	Response	Content
+	arms (Bl)	Hd
+	bone, animal's (Be)	An
+	bones (Be)	An
+	∧> bones, leg (Be)	An
–	branch (He)	Bt
–	fish (Be)	A
–	Florida (Be)	Ge
+	foot, animal's (Be, He)	Ad
–	⌄ head, bird's (He)	Ad
–	hoof, animal's (HE)	Ad
–	humans, whole [may be M] (Be)	H
+	> Italy (He)	Ge
+	Italy, as boot (Be)	Ge
–	leg, chicken's (He)	Ad
+	∧> LEG, CHICKEN'S (Be)	Ad
+	leg, dog's (He)	Ad
+	leg, horse's (He)	Ad
+	∧> LEG, HUMAN ((Be)	Hd
+	∧> leg, piece of (Be)	Hd?, Ad?
+	∧> LEG, RABBIT'S (Be)	Ad
+	leg, rabbit's (He)	Ad

V — D 1 cont'd

+	leg, table (Be)	Hh
+	^LEG, TURKEY'S (Be)	Ad
+	^leg, wooden, human (Be)	Oj
M-	man bowing (Be)	H
+	˅muscles (Be)	An
+	paw, bear's (Ro)	Ad
-	skeletal head of horn (Be)	An, Sc

ATYPICAL
Dl with adjacent Dd of D 4

+	leg and rump, horse's (Be)	Ad

D 1 with Dd 22

M+	LEGS, CHORUS GIRL'S (Be)	Hd

V - D 2

+	bones, animal (Be)	An
-	bottle (Be)	Hh
+	stockings, Christmas (Be)	Cg
-	ears, donkey's (Be)	Ad
+	ears, rabbit's (Be)	Ad
+	elf, human (Be)	H, My
+	feelers, butterfly's (Be)	Ad
M+	figures, two, facing each other (Be)	H
-	fingers (Be)	Hd
+	grenadiers, old (Be)	H
+	hats (Be)	Cg
-	head, animal's (Be)	Ad
+	horns (Be)	Ad
+	˅legs, human [may be M as when described as standing apart] (Be)	Hd
+	legs, table (Be)	Hh
-	paw, cat's (Be)	Ad
+	people (Be)	H
+	sword handles (Be)	Im
-	tree, part of (Be)	Bt
-	water spouts, fountain (Be)	Ls

V - D 4

+	antennae (Be)	Ad
+	‹ anther [s], flower (Be)	Bt
+	bone, animal's (Be)	An
−	∨ carrot (Be)	Bt
+	clubs (Be)	Im
+	∨ cobras ready to strike (Be)	A
+	feet (Be)	Hd
−	fingers (Be)	Hd
+	∨ flower denuded of petals (Be)	Bt
−	hands (Be)	Hd
+	∨ heads, peacocks' (Be)	Ad
+	heads, penguins' (Be)	Ad
+	heads, turkeys' (Be)	Ad
+	legs, bench (Be)	Hh
+	legs, butterfly's (Be)	Ad
+	legs, dog's hind (Be)	Ad
+	legs, knock-kneed boy's [may be M] (Be)	Hd
+	legs, mule's (Be)	Ad
−	roots, teeth (Be)	An
−	ski (Be)	Rc
+	∨ snakes, two, heads up (Be)	A
−	stinger [s], bee's (Be)	Ad
−	animal (He)	A
+	animal part (He)	Ad
+	animal with head cut off (He)	Ad
−	blanket stretched out (Be)	Hh
+	bodies, foxes' (He)	A
+	body, human, lower part of, with leg and wooden leg [may be M] (Ob)	Hd
M+	boy, lying on hillside (Be)	H, Ls
−	brush (Be)	Im?, Bt?
−	bushes (Be)	Bt
−	carcass, animal's (Be)	A
−	cat (Be)	A
+	coat (He)	Cg
+	cross section, hill (Be)	Ls
+	curtain (Be)	Hh

V – D 4 cont'd

+	drapery (Be)	Hh
+	dress (He)	Cg
+	face, bearded man's (Be)	Hd
M+	figure, feminine, reclining (Be)	H
M+	figure, human [usually reclining] (Be)	H
M+	figures back to back (Be)	H
-	grass (He)	Bt
FY+	head, goblin's — a little gruesome because it is more just like a shadow (Bi)	Hd, Ab
FY >	head, large, with little beard, large shiny nose, whiskers stand out (Kl)	Hd
M+	heads, two sleeping men's, with open mouths, large noses and beards (Bl)	Hd
-	horse (Be)	A
+	landscape with clouds (Be)	Ls, Cl
-	leaf (He)	Bt
+	man with wooden leg [may be M] (Be)	H
+	map (He)	Ge
+ >	masks, two, of oriental magicians (Mu)	Oj

+ >	peacock (Be)	A
-	person, whole [may be M] (He)	H
+	plumes (Be)	Pr
+	profile, bearded man's (Be)	Hd
FV+	ravine, down the middle between high wooded hills, as if looking down from the top (Be)	Ls
-	skin, rabbit's (Be)	A
-	smoke billows (Be)	Fi
+	train, costume (Be)	Cg
-	tree, part of (Be)	Bt
FY+ >	tree stump, rotton, covered with moss which is about to fall. Such a decayed nature (Bi)	Bt
+	wings (Be)	Ad
M+ >	woman, arrogant [stretch kinaesthesia] (Ro)	H
M+ >	woman, cautiously bending over (Ro)	H

ATYPICAL
D 4 including D 3

+	boy [may be M] (Be)	H

ATYPICAL
D 4 including D 3 (continued)

+	bird, long-necked, with flaring wings (Be)	A
+	peacock (Be)	A

D 4, upper part

+	face with beard (Bo)	Hd
+	profile, human, with beginning nose cancer (Ro)	Hd, Disease
+	death-mask (Ro)	Hd, Dh
+	mountain range (He)	Ls

ATYPICAL
D 4 including D 3 (continued)

-	bison (Be)	A
-	breast (Be)	Hd, Sex
+	face, any, human (Be)	Hd
+	head, boy's (Be)	Hd
+	head, Satan's, with horns (Be)	Hd, Rl
+	hill (Be)	Ls
-	lambs (Be)	A
+	mountains (He)	Ls
+	profile, man's (Be)	Hd
-	stone (Be)	Mn

ATYPICAL
D 5 with D 11

M+	boy formation, with the folded arms (Be)	H
+	crags (Be)	Ls
+	hills (Be)	Ls
-	humps, buffalo's (Be)	Ad
+	masks, two (Be)	Hd?, Rc?
+	mountains (Be)	Ls
+	^< profile, man's (Be)	Hd

89

+	∨ bowl, fancy (He)	Hh
M.FT	∨ child down at bathing beach, legs bare, the gauzy dress is pulled up by his little arms (Kl)	H, Cg
+	devil with horns [may be M] (Be)	H, Rl
-	donkey (Be)	A
+	elves, human [may be M] (Be)	H, My
+	face (Be)	Hd
+	figure, hooded [may be M] (Be)	H, Cg
+	∧ handle on pair of pliers (He)	Im
-	head, cow's, with horns (Be)	Ad
-	head, deer's, with horns (Be)	Ad
-	head, dog's (Be)	Ad
+	head, human (Be)	Hd
M-	head, human, with two upstretched arms (Ro)	Hd
+	head, insect's (Be)	Ad
-	head, mouse's (Be)	Ad
+	head, praying-mantis' (Be)	Ad
+	head, rabbit's (Be, Ro)	Ad
-	head, rat's (Be)	Ad
+	head with stiff hat (Ro)	Hd, Cg

F-	horns and head, deer's (Lo)	Ad
-	mountain top (Be)	Ls
+	∧< mouth, fish's, open (Be)	Ad
+	nutcracker (LU)	Im
+	pliers (He)	Im
+	∨ vase (He)	Hh
+	wishbone (Be)	An

V-D/

+	animal for dissection, hanging up (Be)	A
+	animal on hind legs (Be)	A
M.FT	aviator in an aviator's suit of leather. The gargoyles are on top of his head. He is looking in the other direction (Kl)	H, Cg
-	backbone of person's body (He)	An
M+	boy, little, pigeon-toed (Be)	H
-	bug (Be)	A
+	child [may be M] (Be)	H
M+	dancer on toes (Be)	H
+	devil [may be M] (Be)	H, Rl
-	dog (Ro)	A
-	doggie (Be)	A
+	duck with mouth open [as duck, D 7 would be −; accent here on D 9 as open mouth, hence +] (Be)	A
M+	girl, show (Be)	H
M+	girl, standing (Be)	H
-	goat (Be)	A
M+	man, back of, on bench (Be)	H
+	Mephisto (Be)	H, Rl

M+	people, two, in dance (Be)	H
M+	people, two, in embrace (Be)	H
+	Peter Rabbit (Be)	A, H
+	^>< rabbit (Be)	A
-	˅shoulder and spine (He)	An
+	snail, seen from the back (Mu)	A
+	soldier [may be M] (Be)	H
-	tree (He)	Bt
-	water of river (He)	Ls
M+	woman dancing (Be)	H

+	bones (Bo)	An
+	bones, articulated (Be)	An
−	∨ hoof, cloven (Be)	Ad
+	legs, child's [may be M] (Be)	Hd
+	legs, person's [may be M] (Be)	Hd
+	letter "V" (He)	Al
+	mouth, bird's, open [with or without enclosed Dds] (Be)	Ad
+	mouth, crocodile's, open [with or without enclosed Dds] (Be)	Ad
+	mouth, duck's, open [with or without enclosed Dds] (Be)	Ad
+	mouth, fish's, open [with or without enclosed Dds] (Be)	Ad
+	∧∨>< pincers (He)	Im
−	plant, open (Be)	Bt
+	scissors (He)	Im

+	antennae, snail's (LU)	Ad
+	beak, bird's, open [with or without enclosed Dds] (Be)	Ad
+	feet, animals' (Be)	Ad
+	feet, bird's, two (Du)	Ad
+	> head, crocodile's, with open mouth (Bl)	Ad
+	flower insides (He)	Bt
+	forceps (Be)	Im, Vo
−	horn, goat's, closed and more bent (Bo)	Ad
+	legs, animal's (Be)	Ad
+	letter "V" (He)	Al
−	mandible, grasshopper's (Lo)	Ad
+	mechanical device (Be)	Im
+	pincers (Bl)	Im
+	pliers (Be)	Im
+	tool and prongs (Be)	Im
+	tweezers (Be, Bo)	Im
−	vase [Ds] (Be)	Hh
+	wishbone (Be)	An

+	bones (Bo)	An
-	coral (Be)	A
-	feathers, long wing (Lo)	Ad
-	fork (Be)	Hh
M	hands raised in air (LU)	Hd
+	head, bird's [with or without enclosed Dds] (Be)	Ad
+	legs (Bo)	Hd
+	legs, calf's, two gnawed (Ro)	Ad
-	legs, deer's (Lo)	Ad
+	legs, human [may be M] (Be)	Hd
+	legs in sport stockings [may be M] (Ro)	Hd, Cg
+	mouth, alligator's (Be)	Ad
+	nutcracker [with or without enclosed Dds] (Be)	Im
-	plants, sea (Be)	Bt
-	snake with mouth open [with or without enclosed Dds] (Be)	A

-	breast, woman's (Be)	Hd, Sex
+	cliff (He)	Ls
-	elbows, person's (He)	Hd
+	face, human (Be)	Hd
+	face, monkey's (Be)	Ad
-	head, dog's (Be)	Ad
-	head, muskrat's (Be)	Ad
+	Indian chief (Be)	H
-	lion (Be)	A
+	man, wild, of Borneo (Be)	H
+	nose (Be)	Ad
+	nose, person's (He)	Hd
+	profile, woman's (Be)	Hd
-	sheep (He)	A
-	stone (Be)	Mn
FV-	trees in distance (He)	Ls, Bt

V - Dd 22

+	arrow (Be)	Im
+	∨ bayonet (Be)	Im
+	bone, animal's (Be)	An
+	bone, human leg (Be)	An
-	branch (He)	Bt
+	cane (Be)	Im
-	finger (Be)	Hd
-	fish (Be)	A
-	head, crane's (Be)	Ad
-	head, ostrich's (Be)	Ad
+	legs, insect's, greatly enlarged (Ro)	Ad
-	∧ limb, dead tree (Be)	Bt
+	machine gun barrel (Be)	Im
+	peg leg, wooden (Be)	Oj
+	serpent (Be)	A
F	snake holding itself rigidly out from rock on which it is. It has tongue stuck out, ready to strike its prey (Kl)	A
+	spear (Be)	Im
+	tail (LU)	Ad
+	tail, animal's, unspecified (Be)	Ad
-	tail, horse's (Be)	Ad

V - Dd 23

+	coastline (He)	Ls?, Ge?
+	∨ face with Russian winter hat (Be)	Hd, Cg
+	face, Santa Claus' (He)	Hd, My
+	faces, false, grotesque (Be)	Hd?, Rc?
+	gnome as gargoyle (Be)	H, Art
+	head, human (Be)	Hd
+	∨ man, old, with beard (Be)	H
M+	night watchmen, asleep (Ro)	H
+	profile with bushy eyebrows (Ro)	Hd

ATYPICAL
D 23 to and including Dd 22

M+	∨ British Redcoat with bayonet behind (Be)	H, Im
+	gargoyle (Be)	Art
+	∨ head, man's, with bandleader's hat (Be)	Hd, Cg

V - Dd 24

+	lady with shawl on head (Be)	H, Cg
M+	person [s] walking (Be)	H

V - Dd 25

+	ᵛcannon (Be)	Im
-	snout, pig's (Be)	Ad

V - Dd 26

+	branch (Be)	Bt
M	phallus, hanging down (Be)	Hd, Sex
+	twig (Be)	Bt

V - Dds 27

+	harbor (Be)	Ls
-	vagina (Be)	An, Sex

V - Dds 28

-	ᵛbell (Be)	Mu
-	V for Victory (Be)	Al

V - Dds 29

+	bay (Be)	Ls
-	foot, child's, in slippers (Bo)	Hd, Cg
FV+	inlet and suggests bay because of the black-white contrast (Be)	Ls
F	lizard, little, creeping, its head raised up (Kl)	A

V - Dd 30

+	dome (Be)	Ar
+	hat, derby (Be)	Cg, Pr
+	head (Be)	Hd
-	penis (Be)	Hd, Sex

- spider (<u>Be</u>)   A

<u>D 1</u>

- skin, donkey's (<u>Be</u>)   A

<u>D 1 with D 4</u>

- meat (<u>Be</u>)   Ad

<u>D 1 with D 6</u>

- animal (<u>Be</u>)   A

<u>D 2</u>

M+ devil, flying (<u>Be</u>)   H, Rl

- emblem, Elk's (<u>Be</u>)   Art

- vertebra (<u>Be</u>)   An

<u>D 3</u>

+ moth (<u>Be</u>)   A

V - ATYPICAL D

upper half entire

- fountain (Be) Ls

W, excluding D 1 and Dd 22 (scored D)

+ insect (Be) A

- joint, human (Be) An

W, excluding D 1, D 2, D 3 and Dd 22

+ butterfly (Be) A

+ cape (Be) Cg

+ robe (Be) Cg

+ skirt, wide (Be) Cg

W, excluding D 3 and Dd 22

- cross section, medulla (Be) An, Sc

W, excluding D 6 and D 9

+ cape (Be) Cg

- caterpillar (Bl) A

+ drapery (Be) Hh

M.FT hammock, in which two old people are lying covered with black woolen rug; they have messed-up hair. Here ["legs"] are the ropes of the hammock (Kl) H, Oj

+ plumes (Be) Pr

D 1, D 11 with adjacent Dd

+ god, Greek, of wind [may be M] (Be) H, My

- rabbits, two, chasing into thicket (Be) A, Bt

- tail and haunches, mouse's (Be) Ad

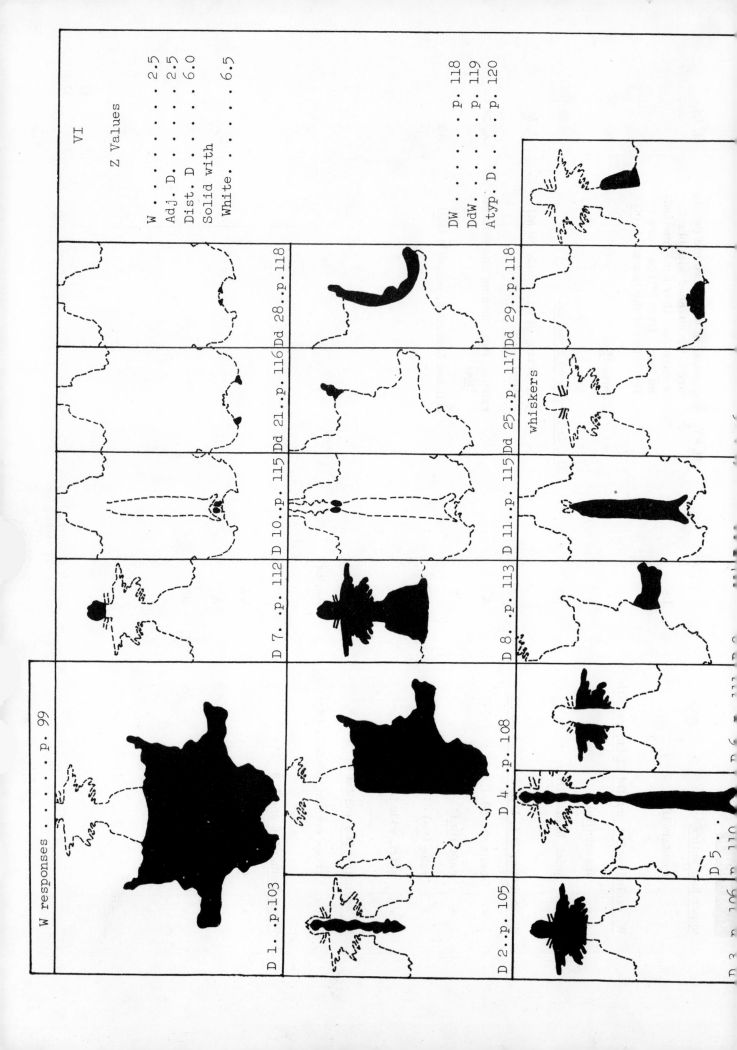

VI

Z Values

W 2.5
Adj. D 2.5
Dist. D 6.0
Solid with
White 6.5

DW . . . . . . p. 118
DdW . . . . . p. 119
Atyp. D . . . . p. 120

W responses . . . . . . p. 99

D 1 . .p.103

D 2 . .p. 105

D 4 . . p. 108

D 7 . .p. 112   D 10 ..p. 115   Dd 21..p. 116   Dd 28..p.118

D 8 . .p. 113   D 11 .p. 115   Dd 25..p. 117   Dd 29..p.118

whiskers

+	> airplane (Be)	Tr
+	ANIMAL BEING SKINNED [may involve T or Y] (Be)	A
+	animal, grotesque [may involve Y] (Be)	A
-	animal, primeval forest [may involve Y] (Ro)	A
+	animal, protoplasmic (Be)	A
-	animal, sea (Be)	A
-	animal, snake-like, on account of head (Ro)	A
-	animal, unspecified [may involve Y] (Ro)	A
-	Australia (Be)	Ge
-	banner, Chinese (Oe)	Art
-	banner, church (Ro)	Art, Rl
-	bat [may involve Y] (Be)	A
-	beetle [head is upper part; legs are lateral projections] (Ob)	A
-	beetle, vague impression of [may involve Y] (Oe)	A
-	bird (Be)	A
-	bird, summer, with long neck (Bl)	A
+	blanket [may involve T or Y] (Be)	Hh

FY-	block, huge marble, an Egyptian colossus (Bi)	Ar, Ay
FY+	blotting paper, smeared, strangely cut [may involve T] (Bi)	Im
-	body, butterfly's (Ro)	A
M+	> boys, two, turning backs to each other [upper section of entire picture heads, and greater part the body of the boys] (Ro)	H
-	brain section (Be)	An, Sc
+	∧∨ bug (Be)	A
+	building with beacon on top (Be)	Ar
-	∨ bullet, high-powered, photographed (Be)	Im, Photo
-	butterfly (Be)	A
-	butterfly, mountain (Ro)	A
+	carriage, Louis XIV (Be)	Tr
+	cathedral (Be)	Ar, Rl
+	chicken's inside, cleaned out (Be)	An
-	chop (Bo)	Fd?
+	church (Be)	Ar, Rl
FY+	> cliff and water, with reflection (Be)	Ls
+	coat, fur [may involve T or Y] (Vr)	Cg

VI

+ coat, sweater [may involve T or Y] (Be) — Cg
+ coat-rack (Be) — Im
- cork with wire through middle, as on champagne bottle (Bo) — Oj
YF cloud, big smoke or soot, bursting out in a jet [light spots on middle line] from a burner ["insect"] (Bi) — Fi
+ club (LU) — Im
+ Cross, covered (Be) — Rl
- crown (Be) — Art
+ crystal form (Ro) — Mn
- cyst stage, tapeworm's (Oe) — A, Sc
+ decoration, hanging, Chinese (Be) — Art
+ desert [may involve Y] (Be) — Ls
+ design (Be) — Art
M+ ˅doll, rag, with arms out (Be) — H, Rc
- door (Be) — Ar
+ ^˅dust-brush [may involve T or Y] (Be) — Im, Hh
+ ˅duster [may involve T or Y] (Be) — Im, Hh
+ ˅dustpan (Be) — Im, Hh
YF+ eruption, volcano (Be) — Ls

- >face, dog's (Be) — Ad
+ ^˅fan (Be, Ro) — Pr
FY+ ˅fan, splashed (Bi) — Pr
+ fish, electric ray (Bl) — A
- ><fish, queer (Be) — A
FY- fish, spread open, the lighter and darker meat (Bi) — An
+ fountain, public (Be) — Ls
- fox [may involve T or Y] (Be) — A
FY- fruit, cut open (Mu) — Bt
+ fur, stretched out [may involve T or Y] (Ga) — A
+ goose, cut open, with feathers [upper lateral; may involve T or Y] (Bl) — A
+ >goose flying [may involve Y] (Be) — A
FV+ gorge in mountain (Be) — Ls
+ guitar (Be) — Mu
- hat (Be) — Cg
+ hatchet, Thor's, two edged (Ro) — Im, My
- >head, dog's (Be) — Ad
+ HIDE, ANIMAL [may involve T or Y] (Be, Vr, Ro) — A

-	hinge (Be)	Im
M+	∨ human, diving (Be)	H, Rc
-	iceberg, floating [may involve Y] (Ro)	Na
+	ice landscape [may involve Y] (Du)	Na.
+	ice sheet melted in sun [may involve Y] (Be)	Na
FY+	icicle on garden pole, covered with frost needles, when it has been melting after cold night [vivid feeling for the object on the basis of the black-white shading with clear appreciation and representation of a quite possible situation] (Mu)	Na
+	insect (Be, Ga)	A
+	insect crossed with snake (Be)	A
+	insect, leaf-imitating (Be)	A
+	insect, spread out, quite flat (Ro)	A
+	∧∨ insect squashed (Be)	A
+	instrument twirling (Be)	Im
-	island continent (Be)	Ge
-	jelly-fish [may involve T or Y] (Be)	A
+	June-bug squashed (Be)	A

+	lamp, table, with beads (Be)	Hh
FY+	∨ landscape reflected in lake (Be)	Ls
+	lantern, Japanese (Be)	Hh
+	leaf (Ro)	Bt
+	∧∨ leaf, maple (Be)	Bt
+	LEATHER [hide] (Be)	A
FY+	∨ legs, spread out, of animal skin. Behind is the tail; everything is spotted and rather worn and old (Bi)	Ad
FY+	lighthouse on rock with light beam [middle section] shimmering on the sea [large gray surface] (Bo)	Ar, Ls
FY+	magazine-rack with torn newspapers; mysterious because of blurred shadings (Bi)	Im, Ab
M+	man whirling very rapidly (Be)	H
FV+	map, aerial, with road down the middle (Be)	Ls
+	∨ map, topographic [may involve V] (Be)	Ge
+	MEAT [animal cut open] (Be)	A
FY-	melon, cut open, or something like that (Mu)	Bt
YF	mold [fungi] on damp wood (Bi)	Bt

VI — W cont'd

+	monster, prehistoric, with snake head and body of a sea animal (Bl)	A
+	monstrance, on top the cross and on the sides the golden tassels (Mu)	Rl
-	moth (Be)	A
-	mountain, big [may involve V] (Lo)	Ls
+	particles with piston (Be)	Im
+	PELT (Be, Ob)	A
+	PELT, BIRD'S (Be)	A
+	pelt, stretched out (Ga)	A
+	person [may be M] (Be)	H
FV+	< picture from airplane (Be)	Ls
-	> plate, crumb (Be)	Hh
+	potato, sick, cut open, with sprouts hanging on it (Mu)	Bt
+	> profiles, two large, with big noses and pointed beards (Ro)	Hd
M+	queen, ancient Egyptian, who gives out orders from her couch (Du)	H, Ay
FV+	river between mountains (Be)	Ls
FY-	rocks (Bi)	Mn
+	rug [may involve Y] (Be, Vr)	Hh

FY-	ruins (Bi)	Ar
-	shark, hammerhead (Be)	A
+	SKIN, ANIMAL'S [may involve T or Y] (Be)	A
+	skin, animal's, stretched out [may involve T or Y] (Ga)	A
+	skin, beaver's; on top it is bursting apart [may involve T or Y] (Du)	A
-	skin, fish's (Be)	A
+	SKIN, LEOPARD'S [may involve T or Y] (Be)	A
YF	smoke rising from a kraal at night; gives you the sense of smell of fires. Smoke barrage. Black spots make it an artificial barrage rather than fire (Oe)	Fi
YF	smoke rising from below and covering everything. One could say it comes from Hell (Bi)	Fi, Rl
-	snowflake [may involve Y] (Be)	Na
+	snowman [may involve Y and M] (Be)	H, Rc
M+	someone who wants to slip into fur coat and gets mad because he can't find arm hole (Bo)	H, Cg
-	star, Jewish (Be)	Art, Rl
+	statue (Be)	Art

VI — W cont'd

+	structure, oriental (Be)	Ar
-	symbol of flag (Bo)	Art
+	tennis racket (Ro)	Im, Rc
M-	˅ thing, diving, arms outstretched, feet together [may be P] (Be)	H
FY+	tombstone, gray marble (Bi)	Dh, Art
+	˅ tree, (Be, Ro)	Bt
+	turtle (Be, Ga, Ro)	A
FV+	valley, coming up (Be)	Ls
+	viola [violin cello] (Be)	Mu
-	wastebasket with handle (Be)	Hh
FY-	˅ whale, lashing water and his re-flection (Be)	A, Ls
M-	woman, knitting (Ro)	H
+	woods [may involve Y] (Be)	Bt
+	worm squashed (Be)	A
FY+	x-ray (Be)	An
FY-	x-ray plate, human body (Bo)	An

-	ameba (Be)	A, Sc
+	ANIMAL CUT OPEN (Be)	A
+	animal's inside (Be)	An
M+	˅ apes back to back on hook (Be)	A
-	bone, hip (Vi)	An
-	book (Be)	Oj
-	candlestand (Be)	Hh
+	˅ coat (LU)	Cg
FY+	coat, fur [because of shadings] (Bo)	Cg
+	∧˅ coat spread out [may involve T or Y] (Be)	Cg
-	cocoon (Be)	Ad
-	creature, winged (Be)	A
YF	death's heads, two, quite black from decay (Bi)	Dh, An
-	door (Be)	Ar
M+	dwarf, holding out hand (Lo)	H, My
-	> face, dog's (Be)	Ad
+	field (Be)	Ls
Y	˅ fire, prairie. Fire and smoke in the distance, as if one were standing on mountain and looking down into valley (Bi)	Fi, Ls

VI – D 1 cont'd

	Content	Code
−	fish (Be)	A
+	FISH OPENED UP (Be)	A
−	flower pot (Ro)	Hh
−	>game, child's, on which marbles can roll around (Bl)	Rc
+	hide, stretched, ox's [may involve T or Y] (Ro)	A
+	˅jacket (LU)	Cg
+	land, piece of (Be)	Ls
FY+	>< landscape and reflection (Be)	Ls
YF	landscape, forest, with many trees. Landslide has come down and destroyed the trees [black stripe in middle line] (Bi)	Ls, Bt
−	landscape from birdseye view with canal in middle and lake below (Bl)	Ls
+	leaf, maple (Be)	Bt
+	leaf, oak (Be)	Bt
−	lobes, two, of the lungs (Bo)	An
−	lungs (Be)	An
FV+	˅map, topographic or relief (Be)	Ge
+	mat (Be)	Hh
FV+	mountains and river, aerial view (Be)	Ls

	Content	Code
+	photograph, microscopic [may involve Y] (Be)	Sc
FV+	picture, rural, taken from hilltop (Be)	Art, Ru
+	rock (Be)	Ls
+	RUG, ANIMAL [may involve T or Y] (Be)	A
+	˄˅rug, any [may involve T or Y] (Be)	Hh
FY+	>sea of ice. Everything covered with ice and snow and entirely deserted. Below the melancholy reflection. Polar solitude (Bi)	Na, Ab
FY+	>shaft, coal, from earth's interior (Bi)	Ls
−	shell, sea (Be)	Na
+	˅shirt (LU)	Cg
+	SKIN, ANY [may involve T or Y] (Be)	A
+	SKIN, ANY ANIMAL'S [may involve T or Y] (Be, Bl)	A
−	star (Be)	As
+	star (LU)	As
−	statue, Egyptian (Be)	Art, Ay
+	stone (Be)	Mn
FY+	˅tank, army, with reflection (Be)	Tr

104

M+	twins, Siamese, together (Be)	H
FY.FT	wig, judge's [center gray], and the little white tabs in front and the fur coat of the judge are hanging on a rack (Kl)	Cg, Vo
FY-	x-ray, chest (Be)	An

ATYPICAL
D 1, from about D 9

+	crown (Be)	Art

VI - D 2

+	beacon, traffic (Be)	Ls
+	boy, Dutch (Be)	H
+	candle (Be)	Hh
+	candlestick, turned wood (Be)	Hh
+	cobra (Be)	A
M+	Crucifix with human (Be)	H, Rl
M-	dancers, two (Be)	H
+	embryo, very young (Be)	An, Sc
+	eel, electric (Be)	A

M+	figure, human, in coffin (Be)	H, Dh
M+	figure, male (Be)	H
-	fish (Be)	A
-	fly (Be)	A
+	god, foreign (Be)	H, My
-	grasshopper (Be)	A
+	head, reptile's (Be)	Ad
+	head and neck, insect's (Be)	Ad
M+	human with arms stretched (Be)	H
-	insect (Be)	A
+	iron core, fountain's (Be)	Oj
+	lamp, street (Be)	Ls
+	lathe work (Bo)	Oj
+	leg, bed (Be)	Hh
+	leg, chair (Be)	Hh
+	leg, table (Be)	Hh
+	mast (Be)	Tr
-	neck, ostrich's (Be)	Ad
+	passage (Be)	An
+	penis, animal's (Be)	Ad, Sex
+	penis, erect (Be)	Hd, Sex

VI – D 2 cont'd

+	penis, human (Be)	Hd, Sex
+	person [may be M] (Be)	H
+	phallic symbol (Be)	Sex, Ab
+	piston (Be)	Im
+	pole, iron (Be)	Im
+	rod, ebony (Be)	Im
-	rodent (Be)	A
+	Russian [may be M] (Be)	H
+	shaft, rotating (Be)	Im
+	snake (Be)	A
+	sword (Bo)	Im
+	thermometer (Be)	Im
+	∨ wood, turned (Be)	Oj
FY+	x-ray, esophagus (Be)	An
FY+	x-ray, woman (Be)	An

ATYPICAL
D 2, with part of D 12

FY+	> mountain range and reflection in lake (Be)	Ls

VI - D 3

-	animal (Be)	A
+	animal with double wings (Be)	A
+	animal with wings (LU)	A
+	asparagus sprout which comes out of the ground (Mu)	Bt
+	banner (Be)	Art
-	bat (Be, Ro)	A
+	beetle (Be)	A
+	bird (Be, Ro)	A
+	bird, two-headed (Be)	A
+	bug (Be)	A
+	bumblebee (Be)	A
+	butterfly (Be)	A
+	coat, fluttering little (Ro)	Cg
+	Cross (Ro)	Rl
+	Crucifix (Ro)	Rl
+	design (Be)	Art
+	design, art (Be)	Art
+	dragonfly (Be)	A
+	eagle (Be)	A
-	fish (Be)	A

-	fish, flying (Be)	A
+	flower (Be)	Bt
+	fly (Be)	A
+	idol, savages' (LU)	Rl, Ay
+	insect (Be)	A
+	insignia (Be)	Art
-	lizard [biology specimen] (Be)	A, Sc
M-	man in swan dive (Be)	H, Rc
+	moth (Be, Ro)	A
+	motif, military (Be)	Art
-	nervous sytem, embryonic (Be)	An, Sc
+	owl (Be)	A
+	penis, winged (Be)	Hd, Sex
+	"pheasant innkeeper" [a contamination of two interpretations of the same detail; the pheasants are the flamelike figures often called birds' wings. The innkeeper is the head of the figure, his big beard formed also by the flamelike figures, and two upward slanting lines on both sides are his mustache] (Ro)	Hd, Ad
+	pigeon (Be)	A
-	plant with leaves (Ro)	Bt

+	pollywog with wings (Be)	A
M+	pope, Russian, who is holding out his hands (Ob)	H, Rl
FY+	reptile, strange [deep black] that is climbing up a cross. Around the cross is a halo; from it is emanating snake-like rays. One can see well the tints of the refracted light, by which the cross is also a little illuminated; only the reptile is quite dark (Bi)	A, Rl
+	seaweed (Be)	Bt
-	shawl (Be)	Cg, Pr
-	snake (Be)	A
+	snake (Ga)	A
+	symbol of death, Egyptian (Be)	Dh, Ay
-	throne (Be)	Art
+	totem pole, Indian design (Be)	Ay, Art
+	weathercock (LU)	Ar
+	wing [s] (Be)	Ad

ATYPICAL
D 3, with D 12 as unit

-	snake (Be)	A
-	tree, pine (Be)	Bt

-	animal (Be)	A
+	ape [may involve T or Y; may be M] (Be)	A
+	bear standing on hind legs [may involve T or Y; may be M] (Be)	A
+	Buddha [may be M] (Be)	H, Rl
-	ᵛbull, bucking (Be)	A
-	^clouds [may involve T or Y] (Be)	Cl
+	ᵛdog, shaggy, standing on hind legs [may involve T or Y] (Be)	A
+	ᵛdragon, legendary (Be)	A, My
YF+	^eruption, volcanic, on the sea. Turbulent boiling water (Bi)	Ls, Fi?
+	ᵛface [s], comic [picture taken from both sides] (Be)	Hd
+	ᵛface [s], Cyrano's [picture taken from both sides] (Be)	Hd
+	ᵛface [s], man's [picture taken from both sides] (Be)	Hd
+	gorilla [may involve T or Y; may be M] (Be)	A
M+	gorilla standing on hind legs [may involve T or Y] (Be)	A
FY+	ᵛhead (Bi)	Hd
+	head, animal's (LU)	Ad
+	head, lion's (Be)	Ad
+	ᵛheads, dogs', with pug noses (Be)	Ad
+	ᵛhuman [s] [any class of or specifically named individual] (Be)	Hd
+	ᵛidols, Hindu (Be)	Rl
-	jungle (Be)	Ls, Bt
FY+	^landscape, dim (Be)	Ls
-	legs (Be)	Hd
+	ᵛman, business, bald-headed (Be)	H
+	mask, with long nose (Be)	Hd, Rc
+	mountain (Be)	Ls
-	><mountains (Be)	Ls
FV+	mountain scene (Be)	Ls
-	pants, pair of (Be)	Cg
+	ᵛrock, geologic (Be)	Mn
FY+	^ruin, somber, on weather-worn rocks. The tower is broken, and there [small projection] it is like a tree cracked in the storm (Bi)	Ls, Ar
FY+	^ship, fantastic [Charon's ferry] and below is the water (Bi)	Tr, Dh
FY+	^ship, icebound (Bo)	Tr, Ls

FY+	silhouette of castle ruin on a rock (Bi)	Ar, Ls
+	^ steamboat with funnel (Be)	Tr
+	>< tank, army (Be)	Tr
M+	v twins, Siamese (Be)	H
FY+	wave, sea, which breaks on prec-ipice in a powerful storm (Bo)	Ls
-	v whale (Be)	A
M.FY+	> woman sitting on mat. She has wrapped black shawl around herself and turned her back. She has child in her arms (Bi)	H, Cg

ATYPICAL
D 4, with lateral half of D 8

+	v dragon, legendary (Be)	H, My

D 4, upper part, including D 9

M.FT	> dancer, modernistic, with one hand way out, the other hand straight up, with great soft robe falling from the arms. Head thrown way back — Martha Graham (Kl)	H, Cg
M+	man stretching out arms; on his head are curls (Bl)	H
+	profile of soldiers' heads with pulled-up visors (Bl)	Hd

+	south coast of U.S.A., including Florida (Ro)	Ge

D 4, lower part, below D 9

FT	faces, two, with soft hood over them, a light beard (Kl)	Hd, Cg
+	v heads, two (Ro)	Hd

+	backbone (Be)	An
+	bone (Be)	An
FV+	ˇcanal from airplane (Be)	Ls
+	canal in female sex apparatus (Be)	An, Sex
+	canoe paddle (Be)	Im, Tr
+	caterpillar (Be)	A
+	column, spinal (Be)	An
+	curling iron (Ro)	Im
+	font (Be)	Ar
-	gate (Be)	Ar
FV+	gorge (Be)	Ls
+	handle, knife (Be)	Im
+	hat-rack (Be)	Im
FV+	highway (Be)	Ls
-	knife (Be)	Im
-	lady [may be M] (Be)	H
+	lamp base (Be)	Hh
+	lathe (Be)	Im, Vo
FV+	lava stream (Be)	Ls
+	leg, chair (Be)	Hh
FV+	ˇmountain range (Be)	Ls

M+	path of projectile [this is a rare non-living M] (Be)	Ab, Motion
+	pencil (LU)	Im
+	pipe (Be)	Im
+	pole (Be)	Im
-	rabbit (Be)	A
+	river [may involve V] (Be)	Ls
+	road [may involve V] (Be)	Ls
+	shaft (Be)	Im?, Ls?
+	shaft, coal (Be)	Ls
+	snake (Be)	A
+	spine and head, bug's (Be)	Ad
+	thermometer, bath (Be)	Im, Hh
+	totem pole (Be)	Ay
-	tree (Be)	Bt
FV-	ˇtrees in photo from hill (Be)	Bt, Photo
+	vagina (Be)	An, Sex
+	ˆˇwater, shooting [may involve Y] (Be)	Ls
+	wood, turned (Be)	Oj
+	worm (Be)	A
FY+	x-ray (Be)	An

−	arms [may be M] (Be)	Hd
+	bird [including specific types] (Be)	A
−	blood vessels, eaten away (Bi)	An
+	branches (Be)	Bt
+	butterfly (Be)	A
+	<cactus (Be)	Bt
YF+	corona of sun (Be)	Na
+	duck (Be)	A
+	feathers (Be)	Ad
YF+	flames, fire (Be)	Fi
+	flames on heraldic weapons (Ro)	Fi, Im
+	geese, flock of (Be)	A
+	gulls, flying (Be)	A
+	headdress, Indian (Be)	Cg, Pr
+	leaf [leaves] (Be)	Bt
Y+	light glare (Be)	Fi
Y+	light, rays of (Be)	Fi
+	mane, flowing [may involve T or Y] (Be)	Ad
+	moth (Be)	A
−	membrane on fish's tail [may involve Y] (Be)	Ad

FY	>mountains, snow (Lo)	Ls
+	pheasant (Be)	A
+	plumage, bird's (Be)	Ad
−	rocks hanging over sea (Lo)	Ls
YF+	solar prominence (Be)	Fi
−	stalagmites and stalactites (Be)	Mn, Na
+	<trees (Be)	Bt
−	vagina (Be)	An, Sex
+	weathervane (Be)	Ar
+	whiskers, animal's (Be)	Ad
+	whiskers, human (Be)	Hd
+	wings, any (Be, Lo)	Ad
+	wings, bird's (Ro)	Ad
+	wings, crow's (Ro)	Ad

ATYPICAL
D 6, projections from

+	beaks, birds', any (Be)	Ad
−	icicles [may involve Y] (Be)	Na
+	turtles (Be)	A
−	wolfhounds (Be)	A

ATYPICAL
D 6, uppermost Dd of

−	turtle (Be)	A

VI - D7

+	animal, microscopic [e.g., para-mecium] (Be)	A, Sc
+	creature with whiskers (Be)	A?, H?
−	Cross (Be)	Rl
+	eyes, mouth, and nose, animal's (Be)	Ad
+	face, human (Be)	Hd
+	face, pansy flower (Be)	Bt
+	features, animal's (Be)	Ad
−	hand (Be)	Hd
−	handle, cane (Be)	Im
+	head, animal's (Ro)	Ad
−	head, bird's (Be)	Ad
+	head, bug's (Be)	Ad
+	head, cat's (Be)	Ad
+	head, cobra's (Be)	Ad
+	head, insect's (Be)	Ad
−	head, owl's (Be)	Ad
+	head, slow-worm's (Ro)	Ad
FY+	⎰ head, snake's, and reflection (Be)	Ad
+	head, tapeworm's (Ro)	Ad
+	head, turtle's (Be)	Ad
−	heads, two bugs' (Be)	Ad
−	nose, horse's (Be)	Ad
+	organ, sex, female (Ro)	Hd, Sex
−	penis (Be)	Hd, Sex
−	people, two [may be M] (Be)	H
−	snout, pig's (Be)	Ad
+	totem poles back to back (Be)	Ay

ATYPICAL
D 7 and upper part of D 2

+	lightbuoy (Ro)	Ls
−	neck (Ob)	Hd
+	organ, sex (Ob)	Hd, Sex

−	animal (Be)	A
−	bell (Be)	Mu
−	bottle (Be)	Hh
+	bug, crawling from cocoon (Be)	A
−	caterpillar (Be)	A
M+	Crucifix with person (Be)	H, Rl
+	dragon-fly (Be)	A
YF+	flames and smoke from volcano (Be)	Fi, Ls
+	fountain with rising and falling water [probably involves Y] (Be)	Ls
+	gravestone (Be)	Art, Dh
−	head, catfish's (Be)	Ad
+	insect (Be)	A
YF+	light with rays and background (Be)	Fi
YF+	lighthouse on a rock (Be)	Ar, Ls
−	monument, fantasy (Bo)	Art
+	monument, war (Ro)	Art
−	mountains, Swiss [may involve V and Y] (Be)	Ls
+	pedestal (Be)	Oj

M+	person sitting on pedestal (Be)	H, Im
M+	person standing on top of hill (Be)	H, Ls
M−	∨ person walking away; you see only the back, bottom of legs (Be)	Hd
−	potato masher, old (Be)	Im, Hh
−	reptile (Be)	A
+	scarecrow (Be)	H, Ru
+	seaweed (Be)	Bt
M−	∨ skirt and bottom of legs seen walking away (Be)	Hd, Cg
+	spire, church (Be)	Ar, Rl
FT	weathercock, carved, with little painted wings, very flat ones. they seem to be trembling delicately in the breeze (Kl)	Ar, Art

VI - D 9

+	arm (LU)	Hd
-	barber pole (Be)	Ls, Vo
M+	> bear, curious, half erect (Ro)	A
-	Blarney Castle (Be)	Ar
-	candy stick (Be)	Fd
+	feet, animal's (Be)	Ad
+	< funnel of steamboat (Be)	Tr
-	head, bird's (Be)	Ad
+	head, dog's (Be, Ro)	Ad
M.FT	> man wrapped in striped blanket with pack on his back, head leaning forward, walking (Kl)	H, Cg
+	peninsula (Be)	Ls?, Ge?
+	person [may be M] (Be)	H
+	rock formation (Be)	Ls
+	sleeves (Be)	Cg
Y+	> smoke (Be)	Fi
-	stalagmites and stalactites (Be)	Mn, Na
+	> tower (Be)	Ar
M-	> woman, old, has her face in hands (Be)	H

ATYPICAL
D 9 and adjacent Dd of D 4

M-	figure, human, female, on lounge (Be)	H, Hh

	VI - D 10	
-	cord section, spinal (Be)	An, Sc
+	eggs (Be)	Fd?, Ad?
+	heads [may be M] (LU)	Hd
+	ˇheads, insects' (Be)	Ad
M-	ˇheads, two, and little hands; people huddled together (Be)	H
-	heart, deteriorated (Bi)	An
+	ˇheart of bunch of rhubarb, which grows in similar fashion (Mu)	Bt
+	jewels (Be)	Mn
-	ˇlabia (Be)	Hd, Sex
+	lips of vulva (Ro)	Hd, Sex
M-	ˇman and woman kissing, affectionate (Be)	H
+	ˇnest, bird's, with two eggs in it (Bo)	Na
-	organ, sex, female (Ro)	Hd, Sex
-	organs, sexual, woman's (Be)	Hd, Sex
+	rear end, animal's (Be)	Ad, Anal?
+	sacks (Be)	Oj?
+	testicles (Be, Bo)	Hd, Sex

	VI - D 11	
-	beans (Be)	Bt
-	birds (Be)	A
+	brain, ape's (Be)	An, Sc
+	brain, monkey's (Be)	An, Sc
+	jewels (Be)	Mn
-	kidneys (Be)	An
-	mice (Be)	A
+	shell, clam's, open (Be)	Na
FY+	street light (Be)	Ls
-	testicles (Be)	Hd, Sex

-	back (Ob)	Hd
-	boat (Be)	Tr
FY+	candlestick with flame (Bo)	Hh, Fi
+	column, spinal, primitive verte-brate's (Be)	An, Sc
M-	dancer, toe (Be)	H
+	flower which has been germinated by seeds (Bi)	Bt
-	penis (Be)	Hd, Sex
+	river [may involve V] (Be)	Ls
+	road [may involve V] (Be)	Ls
-	spear (Be)	Im
+	tree stem (Be)	Bt
+	umbrella stand (Be)	Im
-	vagina, opening of (Be)	An, Sex
+	water of river [may involve V] (Be)	Ls

+	claw [s] (Be)	Ad
+	claws, bird of prey's (Bo)	Ad
+	feet, insect's (Be)	Ad
-	hands, little [may be M] (Be)	Hd
-	head, snake's (Be)	Ad
+	head, turkey's (Be)	Ad
+	horns, cow's (Be)	Ad
+	ice tongs (Be)	Im
-	pincers, crab's (Be)	Ad
+	pincers, little insect's (Ro)	Ad
+	talons, eagle's (Be)	Ad
-	teeth (Be)	Hd
+	tuft of hair on head (Be)	Hd

VI - Dd 25

Score	Response	Content
M+	^arm pushed out of the chaos (Ro)	Hd, Ab
+	^beads from lampshade (Be)	Hh
+	busts, two little (Ro)	Art
+	children [may be M] (Be)	H
M.FY+	fellow, young, leaning against a rock, looking down into the depths. He is wearing beret, and his hair is dressed in the style of a page. Peculiar how the silhouette of the figure and the rock stand out darkly against the background (Bi)	H, Ls
+	ship, forward part of (Be)	Tr
-	>shoe (Be)	Cg
-	stalagmites and stalactites (Be)	Mn, Na
-	toe (Be)	Hd

ATYPICAL
D 25, both, with upper edge of D 1

Score	Response	Content
+	bowl, fountain (Be)	Ls
-	skirt, bottom of (Be)	Cg

VI - Dd 26

Score	Response	Content
+	>Florida (Be)	Ge
-	foot, pig's (Be)	Ad
-	hand [may be M] (Be)	Hd
-	head, dog's (Be)	Ad
+	head, woman's (Be)	Hd
+	heads, eagles', in modern lapidary style (Ro)	Ad, Art
+	Indian chief (Be)	H
+	>leg, animal's (Lo)	Ad
M+	observer, quiet, with crossed arms (Ro)	H, Ab
+	paw, animal's (Be)	Ad
+	person with high Spanish comb [may be M] (Be)	H, Pr
+	antennae (Be)	Ad
FY+	light rays (Be)	Fi
+	whiskers, cat's (Be)	Ad
+	whiskers, insect's (Be)	Ad

VI - Dd 28

- –   claws, crab's (Be)   Ad
- –   feelers, fish's (Be)   Ad
- +   ˅ heads, birds' (Be)   Ad
- +   talons (Be)   Ad
- –   x-ray of labia minora (Be)   An, Sex

VI - Dd 29

- +   profile, king's (Be)   Hd
- +   shoreline, edge of lake (Be)   Ls

VI - Dds 30

- +   cross section, insect pit (Be)   Na
- +   gulf (Be)   Ls
- +   lamp, Roman boat (Be)   Im, Ay

ATYPICAL
Dds 30 and including Dds

- +   nest, bird's (Be)   Na

VI - Dd 31

- +   dogs, prairie (Be)   A
- FY+   moss and snow (Ro)   Bt, Na
- YF.TF   snow, dirty pile of (Kl)   Na
- +   statue (Ob)   Art
- M–   women, kneeling (Be)   H

ATYPICAL
Dd 31, both as one

- –   dinner bell (Be)   Hh, Mu

VI - DW

- –   spider [because projecting D are legs] (Be)   A

DW 3

- –   ˅ crab (Be)   A
- +   insect (Be)   A

VI — DW cont'd

DW 5
- ˅cross (Be) — Rl
- discharge system (Be) — An?, Anal?

DW 7
- body, part of (Be) — Hd

DW 8
- body, part of (Be) — Hd
+ cathedral (Be) — Ar, Rl
+ church (Be) — Ar, Rl

DW 9
- castle (Be) — Ar
+ cathedral (Be) — Ar, Rl
+ church (Be) — Ar, Rl
- ˅cross (Be) — Rl

DW 10
- ˅fish (Be) — A
- lion (Be) — A

- tiger (Be) — A

VI - DdW
+ ice [involves Y; possibly T] (Be) — Na

DdW 21
- lion (Be) — A
- tiger (Be) — A

DdW 25
- castle (Be) — Ar

DdW 28
- ˅fish (Be) — A

outer edge outline D

-	coast of Maine (Be)	Ge

midline D

FY+	carbon poles of electric lamp; between them, the bridging spark [the two bright spots]. There around the light, it loses itself in shades (Bi)	Oj, Fi
FY+	drainage system through meadow; light color around ditch is a sign that most of the water has flowed off from here, if one imagines the water represented schematically by the black color (Bo)	Ls
FY+	fur, recently grown, which blurs in dainty projections into the older parts of the fur, in which stand out single, tight, wooly spots (Bi)	Ad
FY+	tunnel [longitudinal section through] in a mountain (Bi)	Ls
+	zipper (Be)	Im

W, excluding D 3

-	v road sign (Be)	Ls

W, excluding D 6 and D 9

-	v top spinning (Be)	Rc

Z Values

W 2.5
Adj. D. 1.0
Dist. D 3.0
Solid with
White. 4.0

DW . . . . p. 138

Dd 26..p.138
Dd 27..p.138

Dd 21..p. 137
Dd 24..p. 138
Dd 25..p.138

D 11..p. 137
D 9 . . . p. 135
D 10 . . p. 136

D 8. . p. 135

D 4 . . p. 130
D 6. .p. 133
Ds 7 . . p. 134

D 5 .p. 132

D 1 .p. 125
D 2 . .p. 127
D 3 . .p. 128

–	abdomen with pelvis and uretha (Bo)	An
+	adornment, clumsy (Ro)	Art?, Pr?
–	animal cut apart (Be)	A
FY-	bakery goods (Bi)	Fd
–	body, human (Be)	H
+	ˇbowl for flowers (Be)	Hh
+	bread, piece of broken (Be)	Fd
+	bunnies (Be)	A
+	busts, two comical, on stone [if female score P] (Be)	Art
FY+	cactus plant, one sees the meaty joints of the plant quite clearly (Bi)	Bt
–	ˇchain (Be)	Im
+	cheeks, two, of the rump (Du)	Hd
YF+	clouds [response is to figure as whole, or to any details, singly, or in combination, or indiscriminately; content seldom varies, and never much; always scored +; may involve T] (Be, Ga, Bo)	Cl
YF	clouds, storm (Bi)	Cl
YF	clouds, thunder, pressed together (Bi)	Cl

+	clouds, torn, as after thunder storm (Bl)	Cl
+	clouds upon which the God Father is throned (Ro)	Cl, Rl
+	coast line, seacoast [probably involves Y] (Be)	Ls
+	coat-of-arms (Be)	Art
+	ˇcollar for woman's dress (Be)	Cg
+	ˆcoral reef [probably involves Y] (Be)	Ls
+	cover, bed, with flounces (Be)	Hh
FY-	creatures, slimy sea (Bi)	A
M+	ˇdancers, hula-hula (Be)	H
M+	ˇdancers, two, touching each other with their hairdresses behind (Ro)	H
M+	ˇdancers with back of heads together (Be)	H
+	design [any symmetrical motif] (Be)	Art
+	dog act – three on each side (Be)	A
+	dogs, two, balanced on crag (Be)	A, Ls
+	dogs, two, on hind legs (LU)	A
M+	ˇdolls, two, dancing (Be)	H, Rc

M+	∨ fellows, two, who are carrying something, like Atlas (Mu)	H
+	figures, two stone, at an arch, which represent some unknown animal (Bo)	A, Ar
-	flowers (Ro)	Bt
+	fountain [architectural motif; may be Ws] (Be)	Ls, Ar
-	frog (Be)	A
-	fungus (Be)	Bt
FY	fur (Ga)	Ad
+	fur piece [may involve Y and T] (Be)	Cg, Pr
+	game of hammers, where one hammer must always hit the other (Ro)	Im, Rc
+	geopolitics (Be)	Ab
M+	∨ girls, choir, dancing (Be)	H
M+	GOSSIPS, OLD MAID (Be)	H
-	∨ grass plot with shrubs [may involve Y] (Be)	Bt, Ls
FV+	harbor on relief map [Ws] (Be)	Ge, Ls
-	hinge, fanciful [suggested by D 6] (Be)	Im
+	∨ house, Japanese (Be)	Ar

M+	∨ House of Representatives with man making speech (Be)	H, Ar
-	∨ insect (Be)	A
+	island, volcanic (Bl)	Ge
+	isles, sea [probably involves Y] (Be)	Ls
M+	ladies, little, two rococo, with waist and indication of hooped skirt (Mu)	H, Cg
+	lake, outline of [probably involves Y] (Be)	Ls
+	lamp, kerosene (Be)	Hh
+	land with water [probably involves Y] (Be)	Ls
+	map (Ga, Vr)	Ge
FY+	map, geographical, of arctic region, which is surrounded by an ocean [white] (Bo)	Ge
+	map of island with land projections, arranged around bay (Bi)	Ge
+	map of islands, pieces of (Be)	Ge
FY-	map made with India ink, but not well. Continents or something like that (Bi)	Ge
-	mask (Be)	Hd?, Rc?
+	masks, exhibition of (Ro)	Hd

123

FV.FY+	mountains sticking above cloud (Be)	Ls, Cl
+	mouth, cave (Be)	Ls
-	mouth, insect's, dissected (Be)	Ad, Sc
+	necklace, crude (Be)	Pr
+	orange peel (Be)	Bt
+	paper, torn (Be)	Im
+	pelvic organs with sex organ of a woman (Du)	An, Sex
+	pelvis, part of (Du)	An
-	pelvis, woman's (Ro)	An
+	peninsula, relief of [may be Ws] (Be)	Ge
M+	˅people, two, in Russian costume running away from each other (Be)	H, Cg
M+	persons, two [talking, scolding, frowning, etc.] (Vr)	H
FY+	pieces, rising, of cake dough (Ro)	Fd
+	piecrust out of shape (Be)	Fd
-	potatoes, French fried (Be)	Fd
+	puzzle, pieces of (Be)	Rc
FY+	rock, eroded (Be)	Ls
-	rug, animal (Ro)	A, Hh

+	˅scarf, fur, old-fashioned [may involve Y and T] (Be)	Cg, Pr
+	sculpture work (Be)	Art
+	sea growth (Be)	A?, Bt?
-	shrimp, fried (Be)	A, Fd
-	˅shrubs [may involve Y] (Be)	Bt
Y	smoke (Be)	Fi
YF-	smoke, rising (Du)	Fi
-	snow and clouds (Ro)	Na, Cl
FY+	snow, melting [may involve T] (Be)	Na
+	˅stadium [Ws] (Be)	Ar
M+	statue of two people holding part of a lamp [if female score P] (Be)	H, Art
+	statues, two modern Russian, of women (Du)	H, Art
+	stone [s] (Be)	Mn
M+	˅twins, Siamese, joined at head (Be)	H
+	vase, earthenware, just excavated (Be)	Hh, Aq
-	wig (Be)	Pr
+	˅wig (LU)	Pr

VII-D1

M+	WOMEN, TWO [response is to figure as whole, to D 9, to D 2, or to D 1; content varies without end — ladies gossiping, Bridget and Nora quarreling, haughty mid-Victorian ladies; in some instances they are busts, or mounted, on rocks. Scoring on W, or any of D, and on all content variations, is +] (Be)	H	
M+	women, two, scolding. They appear as if jumping out of box (Bl)	H	
−	ˇwomen, two tightly corseted, with only one leg and one head (Bo)	H, Cg	
+	wreath (Be)	Bt	
+	animals, prehistoric (LU)		A, Sc
FT	bird sitting hunched up on branch. It has big feathery fan-like growth on head (Kl)		A, Bt
−	ˇcamel (Be)		A
+	cameos (Be)		Mn, Pr
−	^ˇcat (Be)		A
−	chickie (Be)		A
YF+	clouds [see clouds under W; may involve T] (Be)		Cl
+	clubs, two (Bo)		Im
−	coffee grinder, with lid (Be)		Im, Hh
+	doll, crude (Be)		H, Rc
−	duck (Be)		A
+	ducks (LU)		A
+	dwarf (Be)		H, My
+	ˇelephant (Be)		A
−	England (Be)		Ge
+	^ˇ>< FACE (Be)		Hd
+	FACE, DOUBLE [both D 1] (Be)		Hd
−	face, monkey's (Be)		Ad
M−	face, snarling [D 8 is nose, Dds below D 8 is mouth] (Be)		Hd, Ab

125

−	France (Be)	Ge
+	gnome (Be)	H, My
+	goblin (Be)	H, My
−	goose (Be)	A
+	Gorgon [s¹ (Be)	H, My
+	HEAD, AFRICAN [may involve Y] (Be)	Hd
+	head, animal's (Be)	Ad
+	head, dog's (Be)	Ad
+	head, elephant's, with face and trunk (Be)	Ad
+	head, human (Ga)	Hd
−	head, monkey's (Be)	Ad
+	head, rabbit's (Be)	Ad
+	HEADS [distorted, human, deformed, in stone, rampant] (Be)	Hd
+	heads, two disagreeable rococo, with braids standing up (Bl)	Hd
+	heads, two human (Ro)	Hd
+	heads, two women's, with projecting rococo hairdresses (Ro)	Hd
+	helmet, spiked, ancient German (Mu)	Aq
−	˅ horse (Be)	A

+	Indian (Be)	H
+	jaws, tiger's (Ro)	Ad
−	˅ leg [s], table (Be)	Hh
FY+	map, pretty, of island; towards the shore it declines steeply; wavy terrain — soft tints like one sees on maps (Bi)	Ge
+	mask [s] (Be)	Hd?, Rc?
−	mountain (Be)	Ls
+	Negroes, purest (Ro)	Hd
−	˄ paunch, dog's (Be)	Ad
−	˅ pipe, smoker's (Be)	Im
+	˅ porcupine with tail (Be)	A
+	˅ rabbit (Be)	A
−	˅ riding breeches, with boots (Be)	Cg, Rc
+	rock (Be)	Ls
+	sculpture, modernistic (Be)	Art
−	skunks (Be)	A
+	squirrel (Be)	A
+	statue [if female head score P] (Be)	Art
−	˄ stomach (Be)	An
+	swans (LU)	A

−	swans (Ro)	A
−	tiger (Be)	A
−	turkey (Be)	A
M+	women, or variations [see women under W] (Be)	H

VII - D 2

−	ameba (Be)	A, Sc
+	animal [s] (Be, Lo)	A
+	animal [s], toy (Be)	A, Rc
+	˂bread, fried, in fat [may involve Y and T] (Be)	Fd
YF.TF	bunches, two, of gray cotton, dirty (Kl)	Oj
+	bunnies (Be)	A
−	cat with tail up (Be)	A
+	chairs balanced as in vaudeville act (Be)	Hh
YF+	^v> clouds [see clouds under W; may involve T] (Be)	Cl
+	dog (Be, Ga)	A

−	dog, jumping (Ro)	A
+	˅dog [poodle] sucking at mother's breast (Be)	A
+	^v>dogs (RO)	A
+	˅dogs balancing something on nose (Be)	A
+	DWARFS [may be M] (Be)	H, My
+	dwarfs, two, looking at each other (Lo)	H, My
+	elephant (Be)	A
−	England [British Isles] (Be, Ro)	Ge
+	face, clown's, in papier-mache (Be)	Hd
−	>fox running (Be)	A
−	hair, patriarch's [may involve Y and T] (Be)	Hd
+	head, girl's (Bl)	Hd
+	hind part, dog's (Bo)	Ad
+	INDIAN (Be)	H
+	islands (Be)	Ls
−	kangaroo (Be)	A
−	ˋletter "W" (Be)	Al
−	˅lion (Be)	A

VII -- D 2 cont'd

+	ˇmap of North and South America (Be)	Ge
+	^vmap of Spain and France (Be)	Ge
-	map of United States (Be)	Ge
+	map, relief, of islands (Be)	Ge
+	mountain [s] (Be)	Ls
+	nose (Lo)	Ad
-	pelvis, human (Ro)	An
+	PEOPLE [may be M] (Be)	H
M+	˅person jumping (Ro)	H
M+	PLAYERS, TWO, FOOTBALL (Be)	H, Rc
+	^˅rabbits (RO)	A
+	rabbits with long ear [s] (Be)	A
+	sculpture [if female score P] (Be)	Art
-	sheep (Be)	A
-	shrubs (Be)	Bt
+	snout (Lo)	Ad
+	>statue of diver, badly preserved [probably involves Y] (Be)	H, Art
+	Western Hemisphere (Be)	Ge
M+	WOMEN, FACING EACH OTHER, ANGRY OR EXCITED (Be)	H, Ab

+	WOMEN, or variations [see women under W; may be M] (Be)	H

VII - D 3

-	Alaska (Re)	Ge
+	animal cracker (Be)	A, Fd
+	animal turned around (Be)	A
+	animal, wild (Ro)	A
+	^˅bear [s] (Be)	A
-	˅beehive [s] (Be)	Na
-	buffalo (Be)	A
+	busts, two (Ro)	Hd?
+	candy, cotton [may involve Y or T] (Be)	Fd
-	cat ready to jump (Ro)	A
-	Central America (Be)	Ge
-	˅cornucopia (Be)	Hh
-	cow (Be)	A
+	creature [s] (Be)	A
+	devil with horns (Ro)	Hd, Rl

-	dinosaur (Be)	A, Sc
+	dwarf [may be M] (Be)	H, My
+	face [may be M] (Be)	Hd
+	face, devil's [may be M] (Be)	Hd, Rl
+	face, dog's (Be)	Ad
-	face, goat's (Be)	Ad
+	face, human (Ga)	Hd
+	face, lion's (Be)	Ad
+	face, Punch and Judy [may be M] (Be)	Hd, Rc
+	face, woman's [may be M] (Be)	Hd
+	faces, two, of jumping jacks (Mu)	Hd, Rc
+	> figure, comic [may be M] (Be)	H
+	figure [s], fantastic [may be M] (Be)	H
-	France (Be)	Ge
+	gargoyle [s] (Be)	Art
+	gnome (Be)	H, My
+	goblin [may be M] (Be)	H, My
+	head [s], animal's (Be, Ro)	Ad
+	head, animal's, with forward part of body and paws (Lo)	Ad

-	head, beaver's (Be)	Ad
-	head, buffalo's (Be)	Ad
+	head, devil's [may be M] (Be)	Hd, Rl
+	> head [s], elephant's, with trunk (Be)	Ad
+	head, Fox terrier's (Be)	Ad
-	head, goat's (Bl)	Ad
+	> head, lion's (Be)	Ad
M+	head, man's, evil, deformed (Be)	Hd, Ab
M+	> head of man falling down (Ro)	Hd
+	head, medieval, in stone (Be)	Hd, Art
+	knight, sleeping (Ro)	Hd
+	man, old, laughing (Ro)	Hd
+	> map of South America (Be)	Ge
+	map of Spain [Iberian peninsula] (Be)	Ge
+	mask (Be)	Hd?, Rc?
+	mask, masquerade (Bo)	Hd?, Rc?
-	pig (Be)	A
+	rock [s] (Be)	Ls
TF	rock balancing precariously (Kl)	Ls
+	rock of Gibraltar (Be)	Ge?, Ls?

VII – D 3 cont'd

-	shaving mug (Be)	Im, Hh
-	sheep (Be)	A
-	shirt on line, blown by wind (Be)	Cg
-	South America (RO)	Ge
+	Spain (LU)	Ge
-	U.S. (RO)	Ge

ATYPICAL
D 3, lower, outer corner

+	head, animal's (Lo)	Ad
+	head, sheep's (Lo)	Ad
+	head, wild (Mu)	Hd

VII - D 4

-	airplane (Ro)	Tr
-	animal crouching (Be)	A
-	ape (Bo)	A
-	arch, stone (Be)	Ar
+	archway (Be)	Ar
-	article for masquerade with buckle in the middle (Ro)	Cg, Rc
+	bat, small, with long wings (Be)	A
-	behind, part of person's (Ro)	Hd
+	bird (Be)	A
+	bird, summer (Bo)	A
+	bird with heavy wings (Be)	A
+	bones, hip (Be)	An
-	book, open (Be)	Oj
-	bow (Be)	Im?, Pr?
+	bridge (Be)	Ar
+	butterfly (Be, Ga, Ro)	A
-	caterpillar (Be)	A
-	cats, two (Be)	A
YF+	clouds [see clouds under W; may involve T] (Be)	Cl

VII – D 4 cont'd

−	coccyx (Be)	An
+	cohog (Be)	A
−	cord, spinal (Be)	An
−	fetus (Ro)	An, Sc
M+	figures, winter, bundled up in cape (Ro)	H, Cg
FY	God on the clouds. There one sees the light face and waving hair; oppressed by the black clouds (Bi)	Rl, Cl
+	∧ˇhead, animal's (RO)	Ad
+	hill [may involve V] (Be)	Ls
+	hinge, spread (Be)	Im
+	∧ˇinsect with wings (Be)	A
FV+	ˇland with canal [may involve Y] (Be)	Ls
−	lungs (RO)	An
+	moth (Ga)	A
+	mountains with stream in the middle (LU)	Ls
+	neckpiece (Be)	Cg, Pr
+	painting, background for (Be)	Art
+	papyrus, torn (Be)	Im, Ay
+	pelvis (Be)	An

+	rabbit, lazy, with ears folded back (Ro)	A
+	ribbon (Be)	Pr
+	ˇshell, scallop, open (Be)	Na
+	trade-mark, railroad: wheel with two wings (Bo)	Art, Tr
YF+	water color wash [may involve T] (Be)	Art
−	water-wheel (Lo)	Im
+	ˇwing, butterfly's, damaged (Lo)	Ad
+	ˇwings (Be)	Ad

−	bars, prison cell (Be)	Ar
FT	bird [like pigeon] just sitting itself down on rock, its tail still up, its feathers of whitest color (Kl)	A, Ls
+	caterpillar (Be, Lo)	A
+	coiffure (Be)	Hd
−	čolon (Be)	An
+	comb, high (Be)	Pr
−	dog (Be)	A
+	feather (Be)	Ad
+	hair, flying (Be)	Hd
+	hair, sticking up (Be)	Hd
+	headdress (Be)	Pr
−	horn, animal's (Be)	Ad
−	horn on water fountain (Be)	Ls
−	horn [s], steer's (Be)	Ad
−	legs (Be)	Hd
−	mantilla (Be)	Cg, Pr
−	mountain, Alaska (Be)	Ls
+	mountains extending out into sea (Lo)	Ls
−	phallic symbol (Be)	Sex, Ab
−	pistol, flint-lock (Be)	Im
−	plant (Be)	Bt
+	plume [s] (Be)	Ad
−	potato, sweet (Be)	Bt
−	reptile (Be)	A
−	serpent (Be)	A
Y	smoke (Be)	Fi
−	stalactite (Be)	Mn, Na
−	sword (Be)	Im
+	tail up, animal's (Be)	Ad
+	tail up, cat's (Be)	Ad
+	tail up, dog's (Be)	Ad
+	tail up, squirrel's (Be)	Ad
+	tassel, hat (Be)	Cg
−	tree (Be)	Bt
−	trunk, elephant's (Be)	Ad
−	volcano (Be)	Ls
−	wig (Be)	Pr

+	anus (Be)	Hd, Anal
+	backbone (Vi)	An
+	body, small [may be M] (Be)	H
+	bridge (Be)	Ar
M+	˅ butler with tray (Be)	H, Hh
FV+	˅ canal (Be)	Ls
-	cap (Be)	Cg
-	cap, suction (Be)	Im
+	cleat on boat (Be)	Im, Tr
+	dam [may involve V] (Be)	Ls
+	doll [may be M] (Be)	H, Rc
+	˅ figure, human [may be M] (Be)	H
-	fly (Be)	A
FV+	gateway, beyond a long grove of trees (Be)	Ls, Bt
+	gluteus maximus (Be)	An, Sc
-	˅ groove in chick embryo (Be)	An, Sc
-	hat (Be)	Cg
+	hinge (Be)	Im
+	^˅ genitalia, female (Be)	Hd, Sex
+	lock for canal [may involve V] (Be)	Im, Ls

M+	man in high hat and black coat (Be)	H, Cg
M+	˅ man making speech (Be)	H
+	man, nude (Ro)	H
-	penis, diagram of (Be)	Hd, Sex
-	˅ projectile (Be)	Im
FV+	river (Be)	Ls
-	saddle between mountains (Mu)	Ls
-	structure, organic (Be)	An
-	tree (Be)	Bt
+	twig (Be)	Bt
+	vagina (Be)	An, Sex
FV+	water, running through creek (Be)	Ls
FV+	˅ water and cliffs (Be)	Ls
FV+	waterfall and stream (Be)	Ls
+	zipper (Be)	Im

133

Im	−	arrow (Be)	
Ls	+	bay [may involve V or Y] (Be)	
H	−	body, man's [may be M] (Be)	
Pr	+	bottle, perfume (Be)	
Ls	FV+	chasm (Be)	
Im	F	chopper, old, with chipped away edges, rusty (Kl)	
Ls	+	entrance, cave (Be)	
Pr	+	fan (Be)	
Art	−	figure, plaster of paris (Bl)	
Ls	FV+	gorge (Be)	
Bt	−	grass plot (Be)	
Cg, Rl	−	habit, nun's (Be)	
Ls	FV+	harbor, looking down on a (Be)	
Hd	+	head, George Washington's [may be M] (Be)	
Hd, Rl	−	head, nun's [may be M] (Be)	
Aq	+	helmet (LU)	
(Ls)	+	lake [may involve V] (Be)	
Ls	FY+	lake, little, where on shore the shadow is already coming (Bo)	
Hh	+	lamp (Be)	

−	lamp (Ro)		Hh
+	lamp with base and shade (Be, Mu)		Hh
+	mushroom (Be)		Bt
+	ocean [may involve V] (Be)		Ls
+	pagoda (Be)	FV+	Ar, Rl
	path (Be)	FV−	Ls
+	pot (Be)		Hh
	river (Be)	FV−	Ls
+	stadium, center of (Be)		Ar
+	statue, head of Napoleon (LU)		Hd, Art
+	stone, rocking (Oe)		Ls
−	tent (Be)		Oj
+	tree (Be)		Bt
+	urn (Be)		Hh
+	vase (Be)		Hh
+	water in dish (Ro)		Hh

+	beak (Be)	Ad
+	cliffs [may involve V] (Be)	Ls
M-	devil with spear (Be)	H, Im
+	forehead (Be)	Hd
-	hair (Be)	Hd
+	head, bird's (Be)	Ad
-	head, squirrel's (Be)	Ad
+	horns (Be)	Ad
+	icicles (RO)	Na
M.FY	mosque and people walking towards it – seen from distance; delicate shading (Kl)	H, Ar
+	people [may be M and involve V] (Be)	H
-	shell, sea (Be)	Na
+	snail, horned (Be)	A
+	snout, elephant seal's (Be)	Ad
+	stalagmite (Be, Bo)	Mn, Na
-	teeth (Be)	Hd
-	teeth of dog's mouth (Lo)	Ad
-	turtle (Be)	A
FV+	village on cliff (Be)	Ls

+	animal with human head [may be M] (Be)	A, Hd
+	art, African, primitive (Be)	Art, Ay
+	block in balancing act (Be)	Im, Rc
YF+	clouds [see clouds under W; may involve T] (Be)	Cl
+	> dog [s] balancing object on nose (Be)	A
+	> dogs, two, kissing (Be)	A
M+	> girl jumping (Be)	H
-	head, dog's (Be)	Ad
+	picture done in cross-stitch [may involve Y and T] (Be)	Art
-	pillows (Be)	Hh
+	rocks, piled or balanced (Be)	Ls
-	sideburns [hair] (Be)	Hd
+	stones (Be)	Mn
+	women, or variations [see women under W; may be M] (Be)	H

−	blood vessels, enlarged (Be)	An
−	cat [s] (Be)	A
M−	child in slumber (Be)	H
YF+	^∨ clouds [see clouds under W; may involve T] (Be)	Cl
+	crag (Be)	Ls
+	dog (Be)	A
+	>< dogs, stuffed (Be)	A
−	> face with crown [may be M] (Be)	Hd, Art
M−	football player [s, two] (Be)	H, Rc
−	hat, woman's (Be)	Cg
+	head, dog's (Be)	Ad
−	∨ head, horse's (Be)	Ad
−	>< head, lion's (Be)	Ad
+	hill [s] [may involve V] (Be)	Ls
−	lake [s] [may involve V or Y] (Be)	Ls
+	land [may involve V or Y] (Be)	Ls
−	>< lion (Be)	A
+	pillow (Be)	Hh
−	rabbit (Be)	A
+	rock [s] (Be)	Ls

−	South America (Be)	Ge
+	stones (Be)	Mn
+	support [s] (Be)	Im
−	∨ tree trunks, joined (Be)	Bt
−	twins, Siamese [may be M] (Be)	H
+	wings, insect's (Be)	Ad

VII-D II

+	anus (Mu)	Hd, Anal
-	boat (Be)	Tr
+	∨corolla of flower (Be)	Bt
-	cream, whipped [may involve Y] (Be)	Fd
+	eagle (Be)	A
+	entrance, gate (Be)	Ar, Ls
-	face, man's, seen from front (Bl)	Hd
+	figures, two human (Bl)	H
-	head, goat's, skeleton of (Be)	An
+	humans, two [may be M] (Be)	H
-	organ, sex, female (Bo)	Hd, Sex
+	organ, sex, female (Ro)	Hd, Sex
+	persons [may be M] (Be)	H
+	pier, fishing (Lo)	Ar, Rc
-	river (Ro)	Ls
+	stamen (Be)	Bt
FV.YF-	∨sun setting, with clouds (Be)	Na, Cl
+	wings (Be)	Ad

+	arms (Be)	Hd
-	bones behind the hips (Vi)	An
-	child [may be M] (Be)	H
-	∧face, witch's [may be M] (Be)	Hd, My
-	feather (Be)	Ad
+	garment, piece of (Be)	Cg
+	hand (Be)	Hd
-	head, snake's (Be)	Ad
+	horns (Be)	Ad
-	island (Be)	Ls
-	legs (Be)	Hd
+	paw (Be)	Ad
+	paw, terrier's (Ro)	Ad
-	peninsula (Be)	Ge?, Ls?
+	tail, dog's (Be)	Ad
-	teat, cow's (Be)	Ad
+	∨trunk, elephant's (Be)	Ad
+	trunk, elephant's (Vi)	Ad
-	worm (Be)	A

VII - Dd 24

M+   man, heavily bundled (Be)   H

\+   monkey (Be)   A

VII - Dd 25

\+   halo [may involve Y] (Be)   Rl

VII - Dd 26

\-   body, woman's, cut in half (Be)   H

\-   Christ on cross (Be)   H, Rl

VII - Dd 27

\-   posts (Be)   Im

\+   windows (Be)   Ar

VII - DW

DW 6

\-   pillow (Be)   Hh

DW 10

\-   woodwork, ornamental (Be)   Ar

Z Values

W 4.5
Adj. D. 3.0
Dist. D 3.0
Solid with
White. 4.0

DW . . . . p. 157
Atyp. D. . . . . p. 158
Atyp. Dd . . . . p. 158

Dds 32..p.157

Dd 31..p.157

Dd 27..p.156

Dd 28..p.156

Dds 29..p.157

Dd 30..p.157

Dd 23..p.154

Dd 24..p.155

Dd 25..p.155

Dd 26..p.156

D 7 . .p. 152

D 8 . .p. 153

Dd 22..p.154

Dd 21..p.153

D 2 . .p. 144

D 4 . .p. 148

D 6 . .p. 151

D 1 . .p. 142

D 3 or
Ds 3..p.146

D 5 . . .p. 150

VIII

Note; Determination of color predominance (C, CF, FC) is difficult in many responses to this card without inquiry. The examiner's attention is directed to this necessity by the notation [C?]

Score	Response	Category
+	animals on rocks (LU)	A, Ls
CF+	art, surrealistic (Be)	Art
CF+	∨ attachment for Christmas tree (Be)	Art, Rc
-	basket (Be)	Hh
-	bat (Be)	A
+	bowl [C?] (Be)	Hh
+	brick, ice cream [C?] (Be)	Fd
-	∨ cavity, pelvic [C?] (Be)	An
+	∨ chest framework, human [score P if D 3 is used as spine and ribs; C?] (Be)	An
-	Chinese effect [C?] (Be)	Art
+	coat-of-arms [C?] (Be)	Art
-	coat-of-arms [C?] (Ro)	Art
FC+	crest, Bavarian, with two lions, if the colors weren't different (Mu)	A, Art
+	cross section, anatomy [C?] (Be)	An, Sc
FC-	cross section through chest (Mu)	An, Sc
+	crown [C?] (Be)	Art
FC-	dance around flags (Ro)	H, Art
+	design [C?] (Be)	Art
+	diagram [C?] (Be)	Art
FC+	dish, porcelain, prettily painted with handles [lateral red] and cover [gray] (Mu)	Hh, Art
CF+	drawing, histological, from neurology (Du)	Sc
CF+	drawing, scientific [C?] (Be)	Sc
+	drawing, skeleton [score P if D 3 is seen as spine and ribs; C?] (Be)	An
-	egg, Easter [C?] (Be)	Rc, Fd
+	emblem [C?] (Be)	Art
+	flower [C?] (Be)	Bt
CF+	flower, fantasy, of somewhat exaggerated beauty (Bo)	Art, Bt
+	foliage [C?] (Be)	Bt
CF+	funnel of Hell from Dante; above, ice; below, fire (Bl)	Ls, Rl
-	Greenland [C?] (Be)	Ge
FC-	∨ head, fly's, enlarged (Ro)	Ad
+	headdress [C?] (Be)	Cg

+	ice, fancy dessert [C?] (Be)	Fd
+	Icelandish landscape [C?; may involve V] (Be)	Ls
+	illustration, biologic [C?] (Be)	Sc
+	inside, body's [C?] (Be)	An
-	interior, human body (Bo)	An
+	iridescence, bubble [C?] (Be)	Oj?
+	˅iris [C?] (Be)	Bt
FC	jar, porcelain, with colored designs on it representing various things (Kl)	Art, Hh
CF+	Kreidolf [painter], reminds one of (Bl)	Art
-	man in autopsy [C?] (Be)	H, Dh
FC+	motif, conventionalized, of fairy tale (Ro)	Art, My
+	motif, floral [C?] (Be)	Art, Bt
-	˂object, moving [C?] (Be)	Oj
+	ornament [C?] (Be)	Art?, Pr?
CF	painting, fantastic (Bl)	Art
-	picture of beetle (Ob)	A, Art
+	pyramid, Egyptian (Be)	Ar, Ay
+	print, color, of West [C?] (Be)	Art

C-	rainbow (Be)	Na
+	reefs, coral [C?] (Be)	Ls
M+	Resurrection [shows how the red animals resurge] (Ro)	Rl, Ab
CF-	resurrection of collosal, colored red and brown and blue tumor of head vein [a complex contamination] (Ro)	Ab, An
CF	˅rose, Pentecostal (Bl)	Bt, Rl
-	rugs, animal (Ro)	A, Hh
+	˃scene, mountain [C?; may involve V] (Be)	Ls
+	scene, tropical [C?; may involve V] (Be)	Ls
+	seal, family [C?] (Be)	Art
+	shield [C?] (Be)	Art
+	ship, sailing [C?] (Be)	Tr
CF+	sign, electric (Be)	Fi, Ls
CF-	slide, microscopic (Mu)	Sc
CF+	stain, biology (Be)	Sc
-	statue (Be)	Art
+	thorax (Du)	An
CF	tree, Christmas (Ro)	Bt, Rc
+	tree, Christmas, with presents [C?] (Be)	Bt, Rc

-	x-ray of vertebra, shoulder, lungs [blue gray], and below, the pelvis [yellow] (Bo)	An

VIII - D 1

+	∧∨>< ANIMAL [s] [C?] (Be, Ga, Bl)	A
+	animal, prehistoric [C?] (Be)	A, Sc
+	armadillos (Be)	A
+	BADGER (Be)	A
+	BEAR [S], POLAR (Be)	A
+	BEARS (Be, Ga, Ro, Bo)	A
+	BEAVER [S] (Be)	A
-	> bird with tail drooping [C?] (Be)	A
-	blood system, earthworm's [C?] (Be)	An, Sc
-	boar (Be)	A
FC-	boar colored pink (Be)	A
+	buffalo [es] (Be)	A
-	bug [C?] (Be)	A
-	bull (Be)	A

-	camel [s] (Be)	A
+	∧∨ cat (Be)	A
-	caterpillar [C?] (Be)	A
FC	chameleon creeping along (Kl)	A
+	CHIPMUNK (Be)	A
+	cougar (Be)	A
-	cow (Be)	A
+	coyote [s] (Be)	A
+	CUBS, POLAR BEAR (Be)	A
+	dog [s] (Be, Ro)	A
+	dog, snow [C?] (Be)	A
-	dolphin (Be)	A
-	dragon, Chinese [C?] (Be)	A, Art
+	figures, art [C?] (Be)	Art
-	fish [C?] (Be, RO)	A
+	fox [C?] (Be)	A
-	frogs, conventionalized [C?] (Be)	A, Art
+	gopher [C?] (Be)	A
+	GROUNDHOG (Be)	A
+	GUINEA-PIGS (Be)	A
+	handles, bowl (Be)	Im, Hh

+	hyena (Be)	A
+	hyenas (Bo)	A
-	insect [s] [C?] (Be)	A
+	jackal (Be)	A
-	lamb [s] (Be)	A
+	leopard [C?] (Be)	A
+	lion (Be)	A
+	lion, mountain (Be)	A
+	lizard [C?] (Be)	A
-	lobster [C?] (Be)	A
-	lungs [C?] (Be)	An
+	lynx [C?] (Be)	A
-	man [may be M] (Be)	H
M-	man, who stands there with erect sex organ, but it is too large (Ro)	H, Sex
-	mice (Ro)	A
+	MINK (Be)	A
+	MOLE (Be)	A
+	MOUSE (Be)	A
+	MUSKRAT [S] (Be)	A
+	OTTER [S] (Be)	A

+	panther (Be)	A
-	pig [s] (Be)	A
+	RACCOON [S] (Be)	A
-	ram (Be)	A
+	RAT [S] (Be)	A
+	⌄RODENT [S], CHINESE [C?] (Be)	A
-	salamander [C?] (Be)	A
+	salamander (Ro)	A
FC+	salamander which is climbing (Bl)	A
-	seal [s] (Be)	A
+	sheep (Be)	A
+	sloth [s] (Be)	A
+	SQUIRREL [S] (Be)	A
FC-	>sunshade (Ro)	Im
+	∧∨>< tiger [C?] (Be)	A
+	WEASEL [S] (Be)	A
+	wildcat (Be)	A
+	wolverine [s] (Be)	A
+	wolves (Be, Ga)	A
+	>WOODCHUCK [S] (Be)	A

−	animal, sea [C?] (Be)	A
−	animals, unspecified (Ro)	A
−	∨ bat (Be)	A
FC+	bird, summer (Bl)	A
+	∨ bloomers [C?] (Be)	Cg
−	body, lower part, with female sex organ (Mu)	Hd, Sex
CF+	∨ bouquet (Vi)	Bt
+	butterfly [C?] (Be, Ga, Ro)	A
+	∧∨ butterflies, two [C?] (Be)	A
+	caricature of fat uncle, if there would be added the head and below the legs (Bo)	H, Art
−	chest [C?] (Be)	An
+	∨ cloak [C?] (Be)	Cg
+	∨ coat [C?] (Be)	Cg
CF+	cross section, spinal cord, stained (Be)	An, Sc
−	∨ crown [C?] (Be)	Art
−	∨ dog (Be)	Art
+	dress, child's (Bo)	Cg
FC+	∨ dress, woman's; pink fur with yellow veil around it; sleeves like one wears now (Mu)	Cg, Pr

VIII – D 1 cont'd

ATYPICAL
D 1, both, with D 2

+	∨ flower [C?] (Be)	Bt

D 1, lower half

+	∨ kangaroo (Be)	A

D 1, head Dd

−	face, mummy's (Be)	Hd, Ay

D 1, hind leg Dd, joining D 7

−	leg and foot, human (Be)	Hd
−	tadpole (Be)	A

Score	Content	Code	Category
CF	fire (Ro)	Fi	An
CF+	fire, forest (Be)	Fi	A
+	^v flower, any named variety [C?] (Be)	Bt	Ls
-	fur [may involve T] (Be)	A?, Cg?	An, Sex
-	goods, torn [C?; may involve T] (Be)	Oj	Sc
-	head, lamb's (Be)	Ad	Mn
+	v heads, cows' (Be)	Ad	Bt
+	heads, fishes' (Ro)	Ad	Bt
+	heads, sea animals' (Ro)	Ad	An
-	heads, sleeping (Ro)	Hd	Bt
+	ice cream [C?] (Be)	Fd	Mn
-	insect [C?] (Be)	A	Hh
+	iris [C?] (Be)	Bt	Ls
+	jacket and pants (Be)	Cg	H, Ru
+	v jacket, smoking, gaudy [C?] (Be)	Cg, Pr	Rl, Fi
CF+	jello advertisement (Be)	Fd, Art	Art
VF+	landscape with distant sunset [C?] (Be)	Ls	Sc
FV+	landscape with turrets and forest [C?] (Be)	Ls, Bt	An, Sex
-	leaf [C?] (Be)	Bt	Sc

Score	Content	Category
FC-	lungs, two (Ro)	An
+	moth [C?] (Be)	A
+	^ mountains [may involve V] (Be)	Ls
-	mouth, uterus (Ro)	An, Sex
CF+	nervous tissue, stained (Be)	Sc
+	nuggets, colored [C?] (Be)	Mn
+	orchid [C?] (Be)	Bt
+	pansy [C?] (Be)	Bt
-	pelvis (Be)	An
+	petal [C?] (Be)	Bt
+	quartz [C?] (Be)	Mn
FC+	rag, red, in folds (Be)	Hh
+	^> rock [s] [C?] (Be)	Ls
+	scarecrow [C?] (Be)	H, Ru
C	scene, Hell (Ro)	Rl, Fi
+	v sculpture, cubist [C?; may involve Y] (Be)	Art
CF+	slides, biology (Be)	Sc
CF-	something between women's pants and a skinned pelvis (Ro)	An, Sex
CF+	stain of spinal cord (Be)	Sc
+	stones [C?] (Be)	Mn

+	stones, precious [C?] (Be)	Mn
+	Suit, grotesque (Be)	Cg
C	sunset, red (Lo)	Ls
C+	Sunsets (Be)	Ls
+	Support (Be)	Ab
+	sweet pea [C?] (Be)	Bt
FC+	Vest, Swiss (Ro)	Cg
+	Waistcoat, feminine [C?] (Be)	Cg
-	wing (Ro)	Ad
+	wings, butterfly's (Be)	Ad
+	women, two, wrapped in cloaks [C?] (Bl)	H, Cg

VIII - D 3 or Ds 3

+	BACKBONE, ANY (Be)	An
+	backbone with ribs (Bl)	An
+	blouse, woman's [C?] (Be)	Cg
-	boat (Be)	Tr
+	BONES (Be, Ga)	An
+	caduceus (Be)	Art
+	corset (Be)	Cg
FY+	costume, white ruffled (Be)	Cg
+	deer, little, holding up head. One could even say it is a white deer; very rarely does one find a white deer (Bi)	A
-	face, goat's (Be)	Ad
-	face, human (Be)	Hd
-	face, tiger's (Be)	Ad
+	flower (LU)	Bt
-	flowers [C?] (Be)	Bt
-	head, goat's (Be)	Ad
+	insignia, medical (Be)	Art
-	lobster [C?] (Be)	A
-	pagoda, Chinese [C?] (Be)	Ar, Rl
-	rabbits sitting up (Ro)	A
+	reptile segments (Ro)	Ad

+	RIBS (Be)	An
-	scarab (Be)	Ay
+	SKELETON (Be)	An
+	skeleton, man's (Ro)	An
-	skull, cattle's (Be)	An
+	SPINAL COLUMN WITH RIBS (Be)	An
+	SPINY FORMATION (Be)	An
-	teeth (Be)	Hd
+	thorax (Ro)	An
+	THORAX AND RIBS (Be)	An
+	vertebrae (Be, Ga)	An
+	vertebrae plus ribs (Ga)	An
CF	vessels, man's (Lo)	An

-	children [may be M] (Be)	H
M-	people kneeling (Be)	H
M-	people, leaning (Be)	H

ATYPICAL
D 3, with adjacent Dd

+	drawings, anatomic, with intestines [C?] (Be)	An, Sc

Dds in D 3

-	caterpillars [C?] (Be)	A

Score	Response	Code
–	abdomen [C''] (Be)	An
–	airplane (Be)	Tr
+	animal, sea [C?] (Be)	A
+	animals (Bl)	A
–	animals, two, with heads mashed against each other [C?] (Be)	A
+	antlers, elk's (Ro)	Ad
–	arrow (Be)	Im
+	ᐯ bat (Be)	A
FC–	ᐱ bat, folded up, sucking itself (Lo)	A
+	bodies, stretched, dogs' (Ro)	A
–	ᐸ breast with nipple [C?] (Be)	Hd, Sex
+	BUSH (Be)	Bt
+	butterfly [C?] (Be)	A
+	cap, fur, Russian [may involve T] (Be)	Cg
FV+	castle on hill (Be)	Ar, Ls
–	cloud [C?;Y?] (Be)	Cl
FC+	country, swampy, entry of brook to lake (Mu)	Ls
+	cover, bowl (Be)	Hh
+	crag [C?] (Be)	Ls
+	creature, prehistoric (Be)	A, Sc
–	crest (Ro)	Art
–	crown (Ro)	Art
+	foliage [C?] (Be)	Bt
+	forest [C?] (Be)	Bt
CF	forest, because it is green (Bo)	Bt
–	fur [may involve T] (Be)	A?, Cg?
M+	hands, lady's, who permits her hand to be kissed (Ro)	Hd
–	hands, two, with fingers (Ro)	Hd
+	hat (Be)	Cg
+	head and eye, animal's [white] (Lo)	Ad
–	head, antelope's (Be)	Ad
–	head, elk's (Be)	Ad
FV+	hill, high, with some point on it (Be)	Ls
M–	human diving (Be)	H
M.V–	human with reflection in mirror [Gertrude Lawrence] (Be)	H
+	ice [may involve T] (Be)	Na
CF.FY	iceberg at some distance of bluish gray color, icy looking, transparent (Kl)	Ls

+	ink-fish (Ro)	A
-	insect (Be)	A
-	insect flying (Be)	A
-	kite [fish] (Be)	A
+	lion and unicorn upholding crown [C?] (Be)	A, Art
+	lions, two, quite starved, head [towards middle], legs and tail [towards sides] (Ro)	A
+	mountain (Ga)	Ls
FV+	mountain covered with trees (Be)	Ls, Bt
FC-	mountain, ice, and glacier crevices on a dull day (Lo)	Ls
+	mountain with hotel on the peak (Ob)	Ls, Ar
+	˃ mountains [may involve V] (Be)	Ls
FC+	mountains (Ro)	Ls
+	polyp (Be)	A
M+	pushing together (Be)	Ab
+	rocks [C?] (Be)	Ls
+	roof (Be)	Ar
-	sail (Be)	Tr
-	ship (Be)	Tr
-	skull (Be)	An
+	skull, elk's, preserved (Ro)	An, Sc
-	sunshade (Ro)	Im
+	support (Be)	Ab
CF	symbol [gray] of the upward striving of life, which, however, is being dammed and must flow back. But the canal is too narrow to take everything in so that it explodes. In the middle [darker shadings] is the damming wall (Bo)	Ab
+	tree (Ga)	Bt
+	TREE [S], CHRISTMAS (Be)	Bt, Rc
+	TREE [S], EVERGREEN (Be)	Bt
+	TREE [S], FIR (Be)	Bt
+	TREE [S], PINE (Be)	Bt
+	tree roots (Be, Ro)	Bt
+	tree stump (Be)	Bt
FV+	water streaming down mountain side [C?] (Be)	Ls

−	airplane, cross members of (Be)	Tr
−	blouse, torn (LU)	Cg
−	butterfly [C?] (Be)	A
+	butterfly, new, nice kind of (Ro)	A
+	ᴧᵛcorsets [may involve Y] (Be)	Cg
CF+	crystal form growing out of rock (Ro)	Mn
FC+	cushions, two (Bl)	Hd
CF+	dresses, laundry or something (Ro)	Cg
FC+	flags (Be, Ro)	Art
FC+	flags, two blue (Ro)	Art
−	flower [s] [C?] (Be)	Bt
−	fur [may involve T] (Be)	A?, Cg?
C	grass, suggested by blue, as though it is spring (Be)	Bt, Ab
CF	ice (Ro)	Na
C	ice, color of (Be)	Na
CF+	ice grottoes; the color tint gives that impression (Mu)	Na
+	ice, large cakes of [may involve T; C?] (Be)	Na
+	ᵛjacket, laced [may involve Y; C?] (Be)	Cg
−	˃lake [C?] (Be)	Ls
C	lake (Ro)	Ls
−	leaf, tree [C?] (Be)	Bt
−	leaves, thistle bud's (Bo)	Bt
+	ledge (Be)	Ls
−	lung lobes, two (Vi)	An
−	˄man with huge mouth (Ro)	H
−	map [C?] (Be)	Ge
FC−	map, geographical (Bo)	Ge
−	pelvis (Be)	An
FC−	photograph, astronomical (Bo)	As, Photo
+	pillow (Be)	Hh
−	ribs [may involve Y] (Be)	An
+	rock [C?] (Be)	Ls
CF+	rock, colored (Be)	Ls
+	sails, ship's [C?] (Be)	Tr
Y	satin, beautiful, folds and creases, sort of sheen [may involve T] (Be)	Hh
−	shoulders, man's (Be)	Hd
+	sky [C? V? Y?] (Be)	Na
−	spider [C?] (Be)	A

–	stones (Ro)	Mn
–	sunshade (Ro)	Im
+	treasure, buried (Ro)	Oj?, Mn ?
+	tree, Christmas (Bl)	Bt, Rc
+	trees [C?] (Be)	Bt
–	ˇtrousers (Be)	Cg
+	water [C? Y?] (Be)	Ls
+	wings, two (Lo)	Ad

ATYPICAL
D 5, both, as unit

–	bat [C?] (Be)	A
–	ˇcrown [C?] (Be)	Art

VIII – D 6

+	buffaloes, water [C?] (Be)	A
+	cows [C?] (Be)	A
+	design [C?] (Be)	Art
+	flower, including most named flowers, of wide or round shape [C?] (Be)	Bt

+	flower petals [C?] (Be)	Bt
+	head [looking towards the blue] (Bl)	Hd
+	head, animal's (Lo)	Ad
+	head, ape's (Be)	Ad
–	head, bear's [C?] (Be)	Ad
–	head, bullfrog's [C?] (Be)	Ad
+	head, human, any (Be)	Hd
–	head, lion's [C?] (Be)	Ad
–	head, rodent's [C?] (Be)	Ad
+	head[s], cattle's [C?] (Be)	Ad
+	head[s], lamb's [C?] (Be)	Ad
C–	jelly, strawberry (Bo)	Fd
–	lungs [C?] (Be)	An
+	person, colored (Be)	H
–	potato [C?] (Be)	Bt
+	ˇrock formation [C?] (Be)	Ls
+	rock of Gibraltar [C?] (Be)	Ls
–	sea-lion (Be)	A
+	sheep [C?] (Be)	A
+	simians [C?] (Be)	A

-	bat (Be)	A
-	bird [C?] (Be)	A
+	bloodhounds (Be)	A
C+	blood stains (Be)	Blood
+	butterfly [C?] (Be)	A
+	buttocks [C?] (Be)	Hd, Sex
FY+	canyon (RO)	Ls
FC+	cap, jester's (Ro)	Cg
+	coat, fur, "chubby" [may involve T] (Be)	Cg
FC.FT	coat, woman's, short evening, of some fluffy orange material, whitish rolled-over collar (Kl)	Cg, Pr
+	crystal [C?] (Be)	Mn
-	head, penguin's (Be)	Ad
C+	ice, orange (Be)	Fd
C+	jello, the orange part (Be)	Fd
-	leaves [C?] (Be)	Bt
+	rock formation, mountain [C?] (Be)	Ls
+	rocks [C?] (Be)	Ls
CF.FV	rocky promontory, great cliffs [the great heights at a distance seen to be of orangy stone. They are lit up by	Ls, Mn

-	sassafras [C?] (Be)	Bt
+	shell, sea [C?] (Be)	Na
+	shells, sea, two spiraled [C?; Y?] (Bo)	Na
+	stones [C?] (Be)	Mn
C+	sun (Be)	Ls
C+	sunset (Be)	Ls
FV+	tent, seen from above (Be)	Ls
-	tree [C?] (Be)	Bt
+	wings, butterfly's [C?] (Be)	Ad

–	anatomy [C?] (Be)	An
+	bed, top of, ornate [C?] (Be)	Hh
–	butterfly (Ro)	A
FC.FT	face, devil's. Gray is his fur hat. He has white beard. Wears blue silk coat [face and beard in white] Mongolian looking (Kl)	Hd, Cg
CF	flower (Lo)	Bt
+	flower formation, web-like [C?] (Be)	Bt
+	insect, water [C?] (Be)	A
FV–	lakes with land in between (Be)	Ls
CF–	map of a country with lakes (Bo)	Ge
FC+	merry-go-round (Ro)	Tr, Rc
–	Mother Goose without neck [C?] (Be)	H, A
FC	pines, prickly edges in gray, the blue is glaciers (Oe)	Ls, Bt
FV+	prominence [landscape] (Be)	Ls
+	sailboat [C?] (Be)	Tr
–	shell, crab [C?] (Be)	Ad
+	skate, dissection of (Be)	A, Sc
+	TREE [D 4 must be top of tree] (Be)	Bt

	BACKBONE (Be, Ob)	An
+	backbone (Ro)	An
–	bones, two (Be)	An
+	canal, alimentary [C?] (Be)	An
–	cartilage, vertebral [C?] (Bo)	An
+	column, spinal (Be)	An
+	cord, spinal, insect's (Be)	An, Sc
M–	dancer (Be)	H
+	gearshift lever (Be)	Im
–	mud streak (Be)	Ls
FC	nerve of leaf (LU)	Bt
–	pass over mountain (Lo)	Ls
+	rocket (Be)	Rc?
–	stain, acid [C?] (Be)	Sc?
FC	stick (LU)	Bt
+	torpedo (LU)	Im
FC+	water edge, photograph of (RO)	Ls, Photo

ATYPICAL
Dd 21 with Dd 29

+	pulley apparatus (Be)	Im

153

VIII - Dd 22

	Response	Code
+	arm and finger (Lo)	Hd
-	bodies, alligators' (Be)	Ad
+	hand [may be M] (Be)	Hd
+	hands, two (Ro)	Hd
-	hands, wolves' (Be)	Ad
+	horns (Be)	Ad
-	man [may be M] (Be)	H
+	tree branch (Be)	Bt
+	tree roots [C?] (Be)	Bt
+	wood, dead [C?] (Be)	Bt
+	collar and jabot (Be)	Cg
+	crocus, white (Bo)	Bt
-	flag, inside of [C?] (Be)	Bt
+	funnel (LU)	Hh
+	genital, female, any designations [C?] (Be)	Hd, Sex
-	hour-glass (Be)	Aq
+	labia [C?] (Be)	Hd, Sex
FT	lips, beautifully curved [change in shading shows shape and coloring of the lips] (Kl)	Hd
FV-	mountain, snow-covered, in distance (Be)	Ls
-	mouth, uterus (Ro)	An, Sex
+	neckline on coat (RO)	Cg
FV+	pathway (Be)	Ls
+	river, always becoming broader (Lo)	Ls
+	sticks, golf (Be)	Im, Rc
+	street, little (Lo)	Ls

VIII - Dd 23

	Response	Code
+	arms (Be)	Hd
+	anus (Vi)	Hd, Anal
-	bladder (Be)	An
-	body, lower part, with female genital (Ml)	Hd, Sex
-	bone (Be)	An
-	canoe (Be)	Tr, Rc

ATYPICAL
Dd 23 with adjacent stalk

	Response	Code
+	candle with light [C?] (Be)	Hh, Fi

ATYPICAL
Ld 23 and adjacent stalk (continued)

+	fan, Egyptian [C?] (Be)	Pr, Ay

-	arrows (Be)	Im
+	beak, bird's (LU)	Ad
-	birds [C?] (Be)	A
M+	dancers (Be)	H
+	legs, child's [may be M] (Be)	Hd
M+	man and lady (Be)	H
CF -	monument at night in fog (Bo)	Art, Cl
M+	Peary and Cook (Be)	H
M+	people (Be)	H
-	pincers (Be)	Im?, Ad?
+	pliers (LU)	Im

-	dog lying down (Be)	A
+	fish [C?] (Be)	A
+	island (Be)	Ls
-	lake lost in wilderness [probably involves V] (Be)	Ls
+	rocket (Be)	Rc?
+	stone (Be)	Mn
-	tadpole [C?] (Be)	A

VIII - Dd 26

-	bottle, perfume [C?] (Be)	Pr
-	cone, ice cream [C?] (Be)	Fd
+	∨dog (Be)	A
+	ears, dog's (Be)	Ad
-	elephant (Be)	A
+	∨face, bison's (Be)	Ad
+	head, animal's (Lo)	Ad
+	∨head, dog's (Be)	Ad
-	head, duck's (Be)	Ad
-	head, horse's (Be)	Ad
-	head, man's (Be)	Hd
+	∨head, sheep's (Be)	Ad
M-	man and woman in chair (Be)	H, Hh
-	monkey (Be)	A
FC+	∧∨pillars of colored rock (Be)	Ls
-	shell, conch (Be)	Na
+	∨Sphinx (Be)	Art, Ay
+	turret [s] [may involve V] (Be)	Ar
FC+	∩turtle lifting head over shell (RO)	A, Na

VIII - Dd 27

+	maypole [C?] (Be)	Rc
-	pen (Be)	Im
+	spear (Be)	Im
+	stick (Be)	Bt

VIII - Dds 28

+	∨hen (Be)	A
+	lakes and seas (Be)	Ls
+	∨rooster (Be)	A

+   sea gull [subjective scoring] (Be)   A

DW 1

+   symbol, astrologic [C?] (Be)   Art?, As?

DW 3

CF+   drawing, medical (Be)   Sc

+   bottle, milk (Be)   Hh
+   crutch, part of (Be)   Im
+   pendant (Be)   Art, Pr
+   stirrup (Be)   Tr

+   backbone, piece of (Be)   An
+   caterpillar [C?] (Be)   A
+   club, knobbed (Be)   Im
+   lines drawn (Be)   Oj
-    twig [C?] (Be)   Bt

-    bird [C?] (Be)   A
-    devil [s] [may be M] (Be)   H, Rl
M-   person reclining (Be)   H

W, excluding D 1

Score	Response	Content
−	bivalve (Be)	A
−	body (Ml)	An
FC.FT	bowl that you hang up, out of it growing plant of bluish foliage with a beautiful orange-pink blossom, reminding one of its form, color and delicacy of petals (Kl)	Hh, Bt
−	cave [probably involves V] (Be)	Ls
CF+	creature, marine, of jellyfish order (Be)	A, Sc
+	foliage, mass of [C?] (Be)	Bt
CF+	illustration, biologic (Be)	Sc
FC+	Japanese dignitary: gray hat; the face [intermediate space between gray and the two blue halves] and the clothes [the blue and orange parts] (Ro)	H, Cg
+	∨moss, sea [C?] (Be)	Bt
C.V.	reflection in lake because of color and ripples (Be)	Ls
+	><reflection in water [C?; V involved] (Be)	Ls
+	rocks [C?] (Be)	Ls
+	∨ship sailing through strait [D 5 as sails, D 2 and D 4 as landscape; C?; V involved] (Be)	Tr, Ls
+	x-ray, anatomy [C?] (Be)	An
+	x-ray, chest [score P if D 3 is spine and ribs; C?; Y?] (Be)	An
+	x-ray, "your insides" [C?; Y?] (Be)	An

W, excluding D 2

Score	Response	Content
−	butterfly with wings broken [C?] (Be)	A

D 2, D 4, D 5 severally

Score	Response	Content
+	∧cliffs [may involve V; C?] (Be)	Ls
+	∧edges [may involve V; C?] (Be)	Ls
+	∧>∨rocks [C?] (Be)	Ls

Dd extending into Ds 3

Score	Response	Content
+	foot (Be)	Hd

Z Values

W 5.5
Adj. D 2.5
Dist. D 4.5
Solid with
White 5.0

DW . . . . p. 182
DdW . . . . p. 182
Atyp. D . . . . . p. 183
Atyp. Dd . . . . . p. 183

Dds 32
no responses listed

Dd 31..p. 182

Dd 30..p. 182

Dds 29..p.181

Dd 28..p.181

Dd 27..p. 181

Dd 26..p. 180

Dd 25..p. 180

Dd 24. .p. 180

Dds 23. .p. 179

Dd or Dds 22. .p. 179

Green fingers
Dd 21. .p. 178

D 12. .p. 178

D 11. .p. 178

D 10..p. 177

D 9. .p. 177

Ds 8. .p.175

D 7. .p. 174

D 6. .p. 172

D 5. .p. 171

D 1. .p. 163

D 2. .p. 166

D 3. .p. 167

D 4. .p. 170

Note: Determination of color predominances (C, CF, FC) is difficult in many responses to this card without inquiry. The examiner's attention is directed to this necessity by the notation [C?]

	Response	Content
-	beetle (Ob)	A
CF-	˅ bird-of-paradise [green], with head plume [red], on precipice [brown] (Mu)	A, Ls
-	bivalve, illustration of [C?] (Be)	A, Art
C-	blood (Be)	Blood
-	body. The green is the liver, below in the red is female genital [why liver, color or form? with certainty: form] (M1)	An, Sex
+	body, human [anatomy; C?] (Be)	An
FC-	body, opened from head to thighs (Ro)	An
M+	˅ bookkeepers, two, on high stools (Be)	H, Vo
+	cattle-bears, perfect, which are found in big ocean-lakes. So far as the determinants could be found out -- composed of: bears [the green parts of picture, often designated as bears] (Ro)	A
+	cauldron, witches' [may be M; C?] (Be)	Hh, My
+	chart, medical [C?] (Be)	Im, Vo
+	˅ clothes on a person [Ws; may be M; C?] (Be)	H, Cg
+	corpse, human (LU)	H, Dh
-	cross section, brain (Be)	An, Sc
+	decorative piece [C?] (Be)	Art
+	design for wallpaper [C?] (Be)	Art
+	diagram [C?] (Be)	Art
-	dragon-fly [C?] (Be)	A
CF-	entrance, grotto, with wall scintillating in colors as water runs over them (Bo)	Ls
+	eruption [C?] (Be)	Fi
CF+	˅ eruption of Aetna (Ro)	Fi
+	explosion [C?] (Be)	Fi
CF	fire, glow, and sparks (Bl)	Fi
+	fireworks [C?] (Be)	Fi, Rc
+	flames [C?] (Be)	Fi
+	flower [s] [C?] (Be, Ro)	Bt
CF+	˅ flower-like (Ro)	Bt
+	˅ flowers on hill with brook and pond [Ws; C?; V?] (Be)	Ls, Bt

Score	Response	Category
+	fountain [C? because of water implied in response] (Be)	Ls
-	fungus [C?] (Be)	Bt
CF.Y	gases and flames rising from explosion in which there seems to be also water vapor. Whole thing shooting into the air (Kl)	Fi
+	gladiolus [C?] (Be)	Bt
FC	hat with feathers (LU)	Cg, Pr
-	horns, cattle's [brown peaks], confabulatory completed into cattle (Ro)	Ad
-	islands, connected [C?] (Be)	Ls?, Ge?
M+	˅ lady with parasol [C?] (Be)	H, Im
+	landscape [C?; V may be involved] (Be)	Ls
CF	landscape, fairy-tale: tree, two bushes, there water. Seen from above. The tree of knowledge, of good and evil (Bo)	Ls, Ab
CF.FY	˄ landscape in autumn foliage banking a river and reflected in the lake. You can see the water. The pink is pink clouds (Kl)	Ls, Bt
+	˅ landscape reflected [C?; V?] (Be)	Ls
FC+	light, central [middle figure] that glares and makes figures group themselves around it (Ro)	Ab

Score	Response	Category
+	map [C?] (Be)	Ge
CF	map, colored (Mu)	Ge
CF+	map, geographical, incomplete (Bo)	Ge
+	mask, goblin [C?] (Be)	Hd?, Rc?
-	mess on floor made by animal [C?] (Be)	Anal?
+	movement [may be M] (Be)	Ab
+	object, whirling, with water shooting [C?] (Be)	Oj
C	ocean-lakes, the green spaces (Ro)	Ls
+	orchid [C?] (Be)	Bt
FC+	organs, internal, man's (Du)	An
+	ornament with trees and animals (He)	Art
C	paint smears (Be)	Art
CF+	painting by Stephenson, pastel colors running together (Be)	Art
C	painting, futuristic (Be)	Art
CF+	˅ painting of sunset (Be)	Art, Ls
+	palette, artist's [C?] (Be)	Art, Vo
C	palette of colors (Be)	Art
+	philosophy of life (Be)	Ab
+	˅ pigeons sitting below draperies [C?] (Be)	A, Hh

IX — W cont'd

Score	Content	Codes
+	ˇplant, exotic, with red blossoms [C?] (Be)	Bt
+	plant, marine [C?] (Be)	Bt
CF+	roses (Ro)	Bt
-	rug, animal (Ro)	A, Hh
+	scenery [C?; V may be involved] (Be)	Ls
+	><scenery of sunset with reflection [V?; C?] (Be)	Ls
-	shell, crab's [C?] (Be)	Na
+	skeleton, human (LU)	An
CF-	skeleton with backbone (Ro)	An
-	skull, cartilaginous, in wax [C?] (Be)	An, Sc
C	symphony in colors, quite grotesque (Du)	Ab
CF	ˇtorch procession in garden, glow of the torches passing by, here garden bushes [green] and there a pond [space between oranges]; around that is the ground full of flowers, a peculiar picture (Bi)	Fi, Ls
CF	ˇtree with red blossoms, the top spread out and the stem [middle line]. Around stem, bushes [green], and below, the ground [orange] (Bi)	Bt
CF+	vase with exotic flowers in it (Bo)	Hh, Bt
+	vase with workmanship, and base [C?] (Be)	Hh, Art
CF	Vesuvius when smoke is blown out of interior (Bo)	Ls, Fi
C+	water color (Be)	Art
M-	witches, two dancing (Mu)	H, My
CF	witches with long fingers, dancing over Hell (Ro)	Rl
M+	woman gazing into mirror and reflection [T may be involved] (Be)	H
+	women in costume of '90's [may be M; C?] (Be)	H, Cg
-	x-ray [Y?] (Be)	An

M+	angels, two, with wings floating in the air (Vi)	H, Rl
+	animal [s] (Be)	A
+	animal, blunt-nosed [when muzzle is at midline, i.e., adjacent to Dd 30] (Be)	A
+	animal in water (He)	A, Ls
+	animal, shaggy [T may be involved] (Be)	A
-	animals, or something like that (Ro)	A
-	animals, undersea [C?] (Be)	A
+	ape [Dd 24 as head] (Be)	A
+	bagpipe, torn (Ro)	Mu
-	bear (Be)	A
+	bears (Ro)	A
-	beryl (Be)	Bt
-	bird [s] (Be)	A
-	∨ birds (RO)	A
-	bottle [s] [C?] (Be)	Hh
-	buffalo (Be, RO)	A
-	bunny (Be)	A
+	bust [s], human, with old-fashioned waists [D 2 as head] (Be)	Hd, Art

-	butterfly [C?] (Be)	A
M+	< child, riding on toy [C?] (Be)	H, Rc
M+	> child walking with doll (Ro)	H
+	cloud [C?] (Be)	Cl
CF	clouds (Ga)	Cl
+	∨ coats, women's [C?] (Be)	Cg
M+	dancer (Be)	H
-	> dog (Be)	A
+	dog, Pekinese (Be)	A
-	∧ > dragon [C?] (Be)	A, My
-	elephant [s] (Be)	A
+	face with crown, a stupid fairy-tale king's (Bl)	Hd, My
+	faces, two, Irish (Be)	Hd
-	fishes (Be)	A
-	flower sepals [C?] (Be)	Bt
+	foliage [C?] (Be)	Bt
C	forest (Ro)	Bt
-	frog [C?] (Be)	A
+	gargoyles, grimacing (Ob)	Hd
-	Germany [C? may refer to color on map] (Be)	Ge

163

Score	Content	Codes
M+	girl dancing minuet (Be)	H
+	⌃hares, two, jumping away (Ro)	A
+	head, big, bison's (LU)	Ad
+	head, big, hippopotamus' (LU)	Ad
+	head, cow's (RO)	Ad
+	head, dog's (RO)	Ad
+	head, lion's (RO)	Ad
+	head which is broken in back and opened, cut off at neck (Ro)	Hd
+	heads, hippopotami's [when muzzles are at midline, i.e., adjacent to Dd 30](Be)	Ad
+	heads, sheep's (Bl)	Ad
-	hippopotamus [when muzzle is at Dd 24] (Be)	A
FC+	hunter who is ridiculed by a raven [picture from children's book] (Du)	H, A
M+	⌄Indian crouching [C?] (Be)	H
-	Ireland [C? may refer to color on map] (Be)	Ge
+	jacket [s] [C?] (Be)	Cg
+	⌄lady in fluffy jacket [T may be involved; may be M] (Be)	H, Cg
M+	⌃lady in fur coat, blowing nose [T may be involved] (Be)	H, Cg
M+	⌄lady, old, with cane, crouching (Be)	H, Im
+	land [s] [C?] (Be)	Ls?, Ge?
C	lawn, green (Be)	Ls
CF+	leaves, chewed by beetles (Bo)	Bt
+	leaves, mass of [C?] (Be)	Bt
-	liver (Be, Ro)	An
-	⌃⌄lungs (Be, Ro)	An
M+	⌃man, fat, in silhouette, riding tricycle or motorcycle (Be)	H, Tr
M	man, old, with hat, drinking (Oe)	H, Cg
M+	man with glasses, hair combed back [head seen in motion] (Ro)	H, Im
+	map [C?] (Be)	Ge
-	map of Europe [C?] (Be)	Ge
+	map, relief, with mountain and lake [C?; Y?; V?] (Be)	Ge
C	meadows, large (Bo)	Ls
-	metal, rusted [C?] (Be)	Mn
+	monkey (RO)	A
+	⌃motorcycle rider [may be M] (Be)	H
FC	mountain with precipice (LU)	Ls

-	North America [C?] (Be)	Ge
C	ocean-lakes (Ro)	Ls
FC-	˅peacock [with adjacent Dd] (Be)	A
+	person [may be M] (Be)	H
M+	person creeping along (Be)	H
-	pig [when muzzle is at Dd 24] (Be)	A
+	pig, and similar blunt-nosed animals [when muzzles are at midline, i.e., adjacent to Dd 30] (Be)	A
-	pitcher, water [C?] (Be)	Hh
+	porcupine (Be)	A
CF+	pottery, pieces of, from this color (Be)	Art
+	profile (Be)	Hd
-	rabbit [bunny] (Be)	A
+	˄Rabbit, Mrs. Peter (Be)	A, H
+	rhinoceros (RO)	A
+	rhinoceros [+ only with muzzle at midline] (Be)	A
-	rhinoceros [when muzzle is at Dd 24] (Be)	A
-	rock [s] [C?] (Be)	Ls
C-	Russia [because Russia is green on maps] (Ro)	Ge
C	scene, nature [C?; V may be involved] (Be)	Ls
+	shrubbery [C?] (Be)	Bt
+	skirt [s] [C?] (Be)	Cg
+	South America [C?] (Be)	Ge
-	state [C?] (Be)	Ge
-	Texas [C?] (Be)	Ge
-	thistle (Be)	Bt
-	˅toadstools [C?] (Be)	Bt
-	tree [C?] (Be)	Bt
-	tree bark with sky in background (He)	Na, Bt
-	˅tree stump (Be)	Bt
+	trees, massed, as woods [C?] (Be)	Bt
-	trenches (Be)	Ls
-	˅turkey, fat (Be)	A
FC.FT	urn, Pompeian, made of smooth metal [it is of green color because the metal is now covered with verdigris] (Kl)	Hh, Ay
-	valley [V may be involved] (Be)	Ls
C+	water, green (Be)	Ls

IX — D 1 cont'd

+	whiskers, side, of goblin mask [C?] (Be)	Hd
-	Willow [C?] (Be)	Bt
-	wings (Be)	Ad
-	wings, bat's (Be)	Ad
+	woman [may be M] (Be)	H
M+	woman waving good-by (Ro)	H

ATYPICAL
D 1, with D 4, D 10

+	draperies (Be)	Hh

+	goat (Be)	A
-	head, bird's [C?] (Be)	Ad
+	head, camel's [C?] (Be)	Ad
+	head, cow's (Be)	Ad
+	head, crocodile's [C?] (Be)	Ad
+	head, deer's [C?] (Be)	Ad
+	head, dog's [C?] (Be)	Ad
+	head, elk's [C?] (Be)	Ad
-	head, fish's [C?] (Be)	Ad
-	head, horse's [C?] (Be)	Ad
-	head, monkey's [C?] (Be)	Ad
+	head, moose's [C?] (Be)	Ad
+	heads, reindeer's, with antlers [C?] (Be)	Ad
-	man, prehistoric (Be)	H
FV+	mountain [s] [C?] (Be)	Ls
FC+	rocks, purple, in landscape [V may be involved] (Be)	Ls
-	seal [C?] (Be)	A
CF-	slide, bacteriology (Be)	Sc
-	tree, broken (Be)	Bt
-	walrus [C?] (Be)	A

IX - D 2

+	alligators [C?] (Be)	A
-	beak, rooster's (Be)	Ad
-	castle (Be)	Ar
+	crocodile [s] [C?] (Be)	A
+	face, animal's (Be)	Ad
+	face, dragon's [C?] (Be)	Ad, My
-	face, turtle's [C?] (Be)	Ad

166

+	animal (Be)	A
+	antlers, animal's (Ro)	Ad
-	ape (Be)	A
+	b̌ird [s] [C?] (Be, RO)	A
-	birds (Ro)	A
-	bison (Be)	A
+	blaze [C?] (Be)	Fi
C+	blood smears (Be)	Blood
CF	blood stains, photographed in ar-tificial light (Bl)	Blood, Photo
+	b̌ody, bird's [C?] (Be)	A
-	body tissue [C?] (Be)	An, Sc
+	branch, gnarled, with fruit and suckers, which are growing out of a poorly cut tree (Bo)	Bt
+	caricature [may be P] (Be)	Art
+	carrot [C?] (Be)	Bt
FV+	cliff (Be)	Ls
-	clouds [C?; Y may be involved] (Be)	Cl
M+	CLOWNS PLAYING BALL [C?] (Be)	H, Rc
M+	clowns, two (Ro)	H
-	cow (Be)	A

+	crab (Be)	A
M+	CREATURES LEANING, SQUIRTING (Be)	H
+	CREATURES, MYTHOLOGICAL (Be)	A?, H?
+	deer (Be)	A
-	developmental form [C?] (Be)	Sc
-	dog (Be)	A
+	dragon [s] (Be, RO)	A, My
M+	dwarfs, two, with extended arms (Ro)	H, My
-	face, human (Be)	Hd
+	face with pointed cap (Ro)	Hd, Cg
M+	figures with sabres (Ro)	H, Im
+	fire [C?] (Be)	Fi
-	fish (Be)	A
+	fish (RO)	A
CF-	flames, blazing (Ro)	Fi
+	flower cup [both D 3 as unit; C?] (Be)	Hh
-	GHOSTS [may be M] (Be)	H
+	GIRL [S] [may be M] (Be)	H
FC+	GODS, CHINESE [may be M] (Be)	H, Rl
+	gorge with trees, rocks (LU)	Ls, Bt

167

Score	Content	Location	Code
+	GREMLINS [may be M] (Be)		H, My
+	head, devil's, with horns [may be M] (Be)		Hd, Rl
-	head, human (Be)		Hd
+	heads, moose's [C?] (Be)		Ad
+	heads, Prussians' [may be M] (Be)		Hd
FV+	hill [s] [C?] (Be)		Ls
-	insect [s] [C?] (Be)		A
-	islands (Be)		Ls
+	land, arid [C?] (Be)		Ls
-	lobsters [C?] (Be)		A
M+	MAGICIAN (Be)		H
-	man [may be M] (Be)		H
M+	man, bogey, standing (Ro)		H
M+	MAN LOOKING THROUGH MICROSCOPE (Be)		H, Sc
+	map, relief, with mountains and fjords [V and Y may be involved; C?] (Be)		Ge
+	masks [C?] (Be)		Hd?, Rc?
M+	men, two, greeting each other in unusually polite way [brown bulges in middle are the heads; the antlers, the gesticulating hands] (Ro)		H
CF	miscarriage, preserved; they have such a bloody color (Bi)		Sc, Blood
+	moose running [C?] (Be)		A
FV+	mountain with tree line and trees [C?] (Be)		Ls, Bt
FV+	mountains [C?] (Be)		Ls
-	orchids [C?] (Be)		Bt
+	owl standing on twig (Be)		A, Bt
+	parrot standing on twig (Be)		A, Bt
+	PERSON [may be M] (Be)		H
+	petals [C?] (Be)		Bt
+	pigeons [C?] (Be)		A
-	praying-mantis (Be)		A
-	rat [s] (Be)		A
+	reindeer [C?] (Be)		A
+	rock [C?] (Be)		Ls
+	sand, beach [C?] (Be)		Ls
+	SANTA CLAUS [may be M] (Be)		H, My
+	Scandinavia [C?] (Be)		Ge
-	sea-horse [s] [with Dds] (Be)		A
-	shrimps [C?] (Be)		A

CF+	skirt, orange [both D 3 as unit] (Be)	Cg
M+	SOLDIERS, CIVIL WAR, WITH TRUMPET (Be)	H, Mu
M-	soldiers, fencing, in spiked helmets (Ro)	H
C	sun (Ro)	Ls
C-	⌄sun going down (Be)	Ls
-	Sweden (LU)	Ge
-	thistle, prickly part of (Be)	Bt
-	⌄toadstools (Be)	Bt
+	unicorn (Be)	A, My
+	uphill [V?] (Be)	Ab
+	VETERAN, CIVIL WAR [may be M] (Be)	H
-	whale (Be)	A
+	wings (Lo)	Ad
-	wings, eagle's (Be)	Ad
+	WITCH [ES] [may be M] (Be)	H, My
M+	⌄witches with long fingers (Ro)	H, My
-	woods (Be)	Bt

ATYPICAL

D 3, both, as unit

+	crab (Be)	A
+	plant, insect-catching (Be)	Bt

D 3, with D 2 as unit

-	⌄bird with head turned in (Be)	A

D 3, with D 5 as unit

-	flower [C?] (Be)	Bt

D 3, with Ds 8

FV+	mountains with canyon [C?] (Be)	Ls

D 3, part or all of both, with Ds 8

FV+	canyon with weeds [C?] (Be)	Ls, Bt
+	⌄skirt, open [C?] (Be)	Cg
M+	WITCHES CONCOCTING A BREW OVER THIS CAULDRON (Be)	H, My

D 3, with Dds 23

FV+	mountain recess seen from wigwam [C?] (Be)	Ls

−	apple [C?] (Be)	Bt
−	balls (He)	Rc
+	⌄bust (Be)	Hd, Art
−	chicken [C?] (Be)	A
−	dog (Be)	A
+	doll [C?] (He)	H, Rc
+	∧>∨< FACE, BEARDED MAN'S (Be)	Hd
+	∧>∨< FACE, MAN'S, WITH FLOWING TIE (Be)	Hd, Cg
−	head, bear's (Be)	Ad
+	> head, cat's (Ro)	Ad
+	∧∨>∧ HEAD, CHINESE (Be)	Hd
+	> head, chopped off, with something running out of the nose (Ro)	Hd
+	∧∨>< HEAD, GERMAN'S (Be)	Hd
+	∧∨>< HEAD, GLUTTON'S (Be)	Hd
+	∧∨>< HEAD, HERBERT HOOVER'S (Be)	Hd
+	>∨>< HEAD IN CLOUDS [C?; Y or T may be involved] (Be)	Hd, Cl
+	∧∨>< HEAD, JOSIAH ROYCE'S (Be)	Hd
+	∧∨>< HEAD, LLOYD GEORGE'S (Be)	Hd
+	>< HEAD, MUSSOLINI'S (Be)	Hd
	head, seal's (Be)	Ad

−	∧∨>< HEAD, TYPICAL (Be)	Hd
+	⌄head with pipe in mouth (Ro)	Hd
+	man (Be)	H
+	man in caricature (Be)	H, Art
−	pumpkin (He)	Bt
+	>sponges [C?] (He)	A?, Hh?

ATYPICAL
D 4, with D 10

+	baby [P if D 4 is head] (Be)	H
+	bust of man [P if D 4 is head] (Be)	Hd, Art
M+	>figure, female, sitting on carrier of bicycle (Be)	H, Tr

Score	Item	Codes
-	alligator, baby [C?] (Be)	A
-	arrow (Be)	Im
+	backbone (Vi, Ro)	An
+	backbone, human (Be)	An
+	bat (Be)	A
-	body, insect's [C?] (Be)	A
+	bone (Be)	An
+	∧∨ brook [C?; V may be involved] (Be)	Ls
+	calyx [C?] (Be)	Bt
+	candle [C?] (Be)	Hh
+	candlestick [C?] (Be)	Hh
+	cascade [C?; V may be involved] (Be)	Ls
-	∨ cord (Be)	Im
+	cord, spinal (Be, Ga)	An
+	dagger (Be)	Im
FC+	Eternal Light, moving picture of (Be)	Rl
+	∨ flower stem [C?] (Be)	Bt
CF+	fountain [color of water] (Be, Bo)	Ls
+	fountain-like ascent [middle branch] (Ob)	Ls

Score	Item	Codes
FV+	>< hills, distant, sky and clouds [C?] (Be)	Ls, Cl
FV+	> horizon, town with sky and shore [C?] (Be)	Ls
FC+	incense rising (Du)	Cl
FV+	>< lake's fringe in sunset landscape with reflection [C?] (Be)	Ls
FV+	> landscape [C?] (Be)	Ls
+	life-line (Be)	Im
+	nervous system, embryonic (Be)	An, Sc
+	obelisk (Be)	Ar
-	peninsula (Be)	Ge?, Ls?
-	phallus (Be)	Hd, Sex
-	rainbow [C?] (Be, He)	Na
FV+	∧∨∧ river [C?] (Be)	Ls
FV-	road (Be)	Ls
+	sceptre (Be)	Im
+	smoke rising [C?; V may be involved] (Be)	Fi
-	spit, cooking (Be)	Im
-	staff (Be)	Im
+	stalactite [C?] (Be)	Mn, Na
-	stick [s] (Be)	Bt

IX - D 6

−	animals (Be)	A
−	apples [C?] (Be)	Bt
+	babies, newborn [C?; P if D 4 is head] (Be)	H
+	baby, bundled up [C?; P if D 4 is head] (Be)	H, Cg
M+	ballerinas, four [C?] (Be)	H
+	balloons [C?] (Be)	Rc
+	base, fountain (Be)	Ls
+	base, vase (Be)	Hh
+	bat (RO)	A
−	bird (Be)	A
+	bird (RO)	A
+	∨blossoms [C?] (Be)	Bt
−	boat (Be)	Tr
+	bomb, atomic [C?] (Be)	Im?, Fi?
+	∨bonnet, as in Azores [C?] (Be)	Cg
+	bug (RO)	A
+	butterfly (RO)	A
−	butterfly (LU)	A
FC+	butterfly, red (Bl)	A
+	∧child, wrapped-up (Ro)	H, Cg

−	street over mountain (Lo)	Ls
+	structure, organic (Be)	An
+	sword (Be)	Im
−	tree [C?] (Be)	Bt
+	∨tree stem [C?] (Be)	Bt
−	∨trunk, elephant's [C?] (Be)	Ad
+	tube (Be)	Im
C+	water colors running together (Be)	Color
+	water current [C?] (Be)	Ls
+	water hose (Be)	Im
+	water pipes, two (Be)	Im
+	water shooting up [C?] (Be)	Ls
+	water spray [C?] (Be)	Ls
+	∨water streams [C?] (Be)	Ls

ATYPICAL
D 5, with Dd 22

+	∨tassel hanging from cord (Be)	Hh
−	tree with roots in burlap [C?] (Be)	Bt

+	cloud[s] [C?; T may be involved] (Be)	Cl	Cg, Pr
CF-	clouds, fiery (Mu)	Cl, Fi	
-	⌄collar, woman's [C?] (Be)	Cg	H
M+	dancers, four [C?] (Be)	H	Bt
-	dirt (He)	Ls	A
+	⌃doll baby (Ro)	H, Rc	
-	eagle (Be)	A	
-	earth (He)	Ls	Bt
M+	figures, dancing [C?] (Be)	H	Bt
CF+	fire (Ob)	Fi	Im
+	⌃⌄flowers [C?] (Be)	Bt	Bt
-	ground (He)	Ls	Fd
-	gums, teeth [C?] (Be)	Hd	Color
+	head, human (Ga)	Hd	Ls
+	⌄HEADS, FOUR MEN'S [scored P because D 4 is head; may be M] (Be)	Hd	Ls
M+	⌄heads in whirl [score P if D 4 is separate head] (Be)	Hd	Ls
+	hoopskirts, two girls' [C?] (Be)	Cg	Bt
-	island (Be)	Ls	Sc
CF.FY	⌄jacket, short, pink taffeta, with puffy sleeves. Buttons to hold it in front, whitish feather trimming around neck (Kl)		Cg
+	man [may be M] (Be)		Mn
+	mushroom (Be)		
-	⌄ostrich (Be)		
M+	painting, Degas, of four ballerinas [C?] (Be)		
+	petals, flower's [C?] (Be)		
CF+	petals, rose, falling off (Ro)		
+	powder puffs [C?] (Be)		
-	radishes [C?] (Be)		
-	⌃raspberry sherbet [C?] (Be)		
C+	raspberry stain (Be)		
-	⌃reservoir [water] (Be)		
+	⌃⌄rocks [C?] (Be)		
-	rocks (LU)		
+	roses, pink [C?] (Be)		
CF-	⌄section in microscope (Be)		
+	skirt [C?] (Be)		
+	stones [C?] (Be)		

IX — D 6 cont'd

Score	Response	Content
+	eagles (Be)	A
+	feelers, bug's [C?] (Be)	Ad
+	figure, little female, sitting and looking out onto lake (Ro)	H, Ls
M+	^>< girl, figure-skating (Be)	H, Rc
+	growth, vegetable [C?] (Be)	Bt
+	gun, machine (Be)	Im
+	hands [may be M] (Be)	Hd
+	horn (Be)	Mu
+	horn, animal's [C?] (Be)	Ad
+	leg, bird's [C?] (Be)	Ad
-	map, Mediterranean portion of [C?] (Be)	Ge
M+	^>< person falling (Be)	H
M+	^>< person jumping (Be)	H
M+	^>< person running (Be)	H
+	> persons trying to climb cliff (He)	H
+	picture of people [often seen this way, occasionally in motion; in this case no movement] (Ro)	H
M+	^>< pirates digging gold [C?] (Be)	H
+	root-stocks (Mu)	Bt
+	∨ roots (Be)	Bt
C	sunset (Be)	Ls
+	∨ tree (Du)	Bt
FC+	∨ tree, red peach (Bl)	Bt
-	water (He)	Ls
-	wings on caterpillar [C?] (Be)	Ad

ATYPICAL
D 6, half of

Score	Response	Content	
+	∧ baby [score P if D 4 is head] (Be)	H	∨

IX - D 7

Score	Response	Content
+	antennae, two (Lo)	Ad
+	antlers [C?] (Be, Lo)	Ad
+	arm, statue (Be)	Hd, Art
+	∨ bones connected (Be)	An
+	claw [s], crab's [C?] (Be, Bo)	Ad
+	claw, lobster's [C?] (Be)	Ad
+	designs, paper, to cut out for children (He)	Art, Rc
-	dog, digging, rear of (Be)	Ad

Sign	Response	Code
+	ˇroots, feed (Be)	Bt
+	snail with horns (Lo)	A
-	sword (Be)	Im
+	telescopes (Be)	Im
-	tiger (Lo)	A
+	∧∨ tree (Be)	Bt
+	tree branches (Be)	Bt
-	wings (Be)	Ad

ATYPICAL
D 7, both, with Dd 25 as unit

Sign	Response	Code
-	arch [V may be involved] (Be)	Ar
+	bridge [V may be involved] (Be)	Ar
-	gate [V may be involved] (Be)	Ar

Sign	Response	Code
-	animal (Be)	A
-	bell (Be)	Mu
+	ˇbust (Ro)	Art
+	canyon [V?] (Be)	Ls
+	cello (Be)	Mu
+	chalice with host (Bo)	Rl
+	chandelier (Be)	Hh
+	ˇchasm [V?] (Be)	Ls
+	design [C?] (Be)	Art
+	dress [C?] (Be)	Cg
FY.FT	ˇelectric bulb, white, frosted [shadings make it appear so] (Kl)	Hh
-	ˇelephant [front elevation] (Be)	A
CF-	entrance, cave (Ro)	Ls
+	fiddle, bull (Be)	Mu
+	garden vista [V?; C?] (Be)	Ls
+	glass, cocktail (Be)	Hh
+	globe for fish [C?] (Be)	Hh
+	goblet (Bo)	Hh
+	guitar with strings in middle (Mu)	Mu

175

-	ˇhead, creature's (Be)	Ad
+	head, ink-fish's, seen from above (Bl)	Ad
+	hole [V may be involved] (Be)	Ls
+	hour-glass (Be)	Aq
-	kettle (Be)	Hh
-	keyhole (Be)	Hh
+	><lake [C?] (Be)	Ls
+	>lake with diving board [C?] (Be)	Ls, Rc
+	><landscape [various, e.g., with water, distant hills, sky, clouds; V?; C?] (Be)	Ls
M-	ˇman, funny (Be)	H
FC+	man, snow, fat (Bi)	H, Rc
+	mushroom (Bo)	Bt
+	picture under water [C?] (Be)	Ls
+	ˇpond [C?] (Be)	Ls
-	screwdriver holder (Be)	Im
Y	snow (Be)	Na
Y	snow mountain [V may be involved] (Be)	Na
+	top, bottle (Be)	Hh
-	top, plumb line (Be)	Im
+	spool or something like that (Mu)	Oj
+	urn (Be)	Hh
+	vase (Bo)	Hh
+	ˆˇvase, fancy [C?] (Be)	Hh
+	ventilator on ship (Be)	Tr
+	violin (Be, Ro)	Mu
+	water [C?] (Be)	Ls
+	woman [or any feminine form; may be M] (Be)	H

	Response	Code
+	bomb, atomic [C?] (Be)	Im?, Fi?
+	explosion [C?] (Be)	Fi
+	˅flower [C?] (Be)	Bt
+	fountain (Be)	Ls
+	˅lampshade [C?] (Be)	Hh
+	merry-go-round [C?] (Be)	Rc
+	˅mushrooms [C?] (Be)	Bt
+	˅parasol, pink [C?] (Be)	Im, Pr
-	spindle, office (Be)	Im
+	˅tree, catalpa, pink [C?] (Be)	Bt
+	˅umbrella [C?] (Be)	Im

ATYPICAL

D 9, with D 1 as unit

	Response	Code
+	tree, shaded [C?] (Be)	Bt

D 9, with D 3

	Response	Code
+	˄water reservoir with pipes and dead earth [C?] (Be)	Ls, Im

D 9, with Ds 8

	Response	Code
+	vase on stand [C?] (Be)	Hh

	Response	Code
-	animal [C?] (Be)	A
+	bird [s] [C?] (Be)	A
+	buttocks (Be)	Hd
-	face [s] [may be M] (Be)	Hd
-	head [s] [may be M] (Be)	Hd
-	heads [when D 10 is separately selected; scored + only when included in D 6 as four heads] (Be)	Hd
-	heads, babies' [may be M] (Be)	Hd
+	˅heads, elephants' (Be)	Ad
+	penguins (Be)	A
+	poppies [C?] (Be)	Bt
+	rock [C?] (Be)	Ls
+	ruffles, dress [C?] (Be)	Cg, Pr
-	tree roots in burlap (Be)	Bt
+	tulip [C?] (Be)	Bt

IX - D 11

+	bat (Be, RO)	A
+	bird (RO)	A
+	butterfly [C?] (Be, RO)	A
-	cradle (Be)	Hh
-	cup (Be)	Hh
+	insect (RO)	A
+	pelvis (Be)	An
-	ˇrock [C?] (Be)	Ls

IX - Dd 21

+	claws (Be)	Ad
+	fingers [may be M] (Be)	Hd
-	guns, machine, four (Be)	Im
+	hands [may be M] (Be)	Hd
M+	hands, leaning on something (Be)	Hd
-	keys, piano [with Dds] (Be)	Mu
-	nerves, teeth (Be)	An
-	spears, four (Be)	Im
-	teeth (Be)	Hd?, Ad?
+	toes (Be)	Hd

IX - D 12

-	chicken being cooked (Be)	A, Fd
-	fungus [C?] (Be)	Bt
FC+	gods, Chinese, with masks and flowing skirts (Be)	H, Rl
+	<landscape [C?; V may be involved] (Be)	Ls
-	toadstools [C?] (Be)	Bt
-	ˇtree (Be)	Bt
+	workmanship on vase [C?] (Be)	Hh, Art
-	x-ray [Y may be involved] (Be)	An

+	apple, half, with the stones (LU)	Bt
-	Bering Sea (Be)	Ge
+	bridge [may involve V] (Be)	Ar
CF+	button, iron, with rust and verdigris on top (Mu)	Oj
+	cavern [may involve V] (Be)	Ls
V	depth, looking down into cavern (Be)	Ls, Ab
-	doors, swinging (Be)	Ar
+	eyes, goblin mask [C?] (Be)	Hd, Rc
+	eyes, monster's (Be)	Ad
-	fish (Be)	A
+	garden, terraced [V?] (Be)	Ls
-	head, flatfish's (Be)	Ad
-	head, fly's (Be)	Ad
-	jellyfish [C?] (Be)	A
+	jellyfish (Ro)	A
+	lake [C?] (Be, He)	Ls
+	mushroom [C?] (Be)	Bt
-	owl (LU)	A
+	ponds [C?] (Be)	Ls
-	skull (Be)	An

+	ball in black and white (He)	Rc
+	eyes [Y may be involved] (Be)	Hd?, Ad?
-	eyes (Bl)	Hd
+	eyes, pumpkin's (He)	Bt, Rc
+	holes for animal's home [V may be involved] (Be)	Ls
+	holes shot through [V may be involved] (Be)	Oj
FV+	hollows, two little (Be)	Oj
-	island (Be)	Ls
-	kidneys (Ro)	An
+	lake in mountains (He)	Ls
-	moon, quarter-, rising (Be)	As
+	moon with shaded parts (He)	As
-	mouth (Be)	Hd?, Ad?
-	nostrils, horse's, dilated [Y may be involved] (Be)	Ad
+	ponds (Be)	Ls
-	shell, oyster's (Be)	Na
+	slits in canvas [V may be involved] (Be)	Oj
+	tunnels (He)	Ls
+	windows (Be)	Ar

IX - Dd 24

+	face, animal's (Be)	Ad
-	face, human [when outer edge is profile] (Be)	Hd
+	head, camel's (Be)	Ad
+	head, ram's (Be)	Ad

ATYPICAL
Dd 25, with Dds 32

+	cross section, eye [Y may be involved] (Be)	An, Sc
+	ice-cream cone [C?; Y may be involved] (Be)	Fd
+	iris of eyeball [Y may be involved] (Be)	Hd

IX - Dd 25

-	archway [both Dd 25 as unit; V may be involved] (Be)	Ar
+	bridge [both Dd 25 as unit; V may be involved] (Be)	Ar
-	dome, building [usually both Dd 25 as unit] (Be)	Ar
-	dome, temple [usually both Dd 25 as unit] (Be)	Ar, Rl
+	liquid, squirted (Be)	Oj
+	northern lights [Y may be involved] (Be)	Na
+	smoke from gun [C?; Y may be involved] (Be)	Fi

IX - Dd 26

+	boat (Be)	Tr
-	bugle (Be)	Mu
-	dog (Be)	A
+	⌐farmer [may be M] (Be)	H, Ru
M+	⌐football player, punting (Be)	H, Rc
+	guns (Be)	Im
-	horn (Be)	Mu
+	⌃man [may be M] (Be)	H
-	nose (Be)	Hd?, Ad?
-	saw (Be)	Im
+	woman [may be M] (Be)	H

ATYPICAL
Dd 26 and 27

M	>Someone taking water out of pail (Be)	H

IX - Dd 27

–	angelfish (Be)	A
–	animal (Be)	A
–	bull (Be)	A
–	head, dog's (Be)	Ad
M+	<lady, old-fashioned, with basket (Be)	H
+	>man [may be M] (Be)	H
–	penguin (Be)	A
+	person [may be M] (Be)	H
–	squirrel (Be)	A
+	woman [may be M] (Be)	H

–	Alaska [C? may refer to map color] (Be)	Ge
C–	blood splotches (Be)	Blood
–	dog (Be)	A
–	moss [C?; Y may be involved] (Be)	Bt
–	owls, two (Ro)	A
+	stomach [C?] (Be)	An
–	wing, airplane (RO)	Tr

IX - Dds 29

–	bell (Be)	Mu
+	Caspian Sea [Y may be involved] (Be)	Ge
–	face, lady's (Be)	Hd
–	Greenland (Be)	Ge
–	head, Punch and Judy (Be)	Hd, Rc
+	lake [Y may be involved] (Be)	Ls
–	man [may be M] (Be)	H
–	>North America [Y may be involved] (Be)	Ge

IX — Dds 29 cont'd

- triangle (Be) — Im?
- watershed, Hudson's Bay [Y may be involved] (Be) — Ls?, Ge?

IX - Dd 31

+ face (Be) — Hd

IX - Dd 30

- alligator [C?] (Be) — A
CF+ blood, drops of (Be) — Blood
- body, caterpillar's [C?] (Be) — A
FC+ branch, budding, beautiful, of cherry tree in spring (Mu) — Bt
M+ cross and boy tied to it [C?] (Ro) — H, Rl
M- dancers, Adagio (Be) — H
M.FT fetish, little, of carved wood showing a stylized figure, hand folded in front (Kl) — H, Art
- penis (Be) — Hd, Sex
+ shinbone (Be) — An
+ tallow, dripping (Be) — Hh
+ tears from crying (Be) — ?
- tree root (Be) — Bt

IX - DW

DW 3
- body, headless [may be M] (Be) — Hd

DW 5
- body, headless [may be M] (Be) — Hd

DW 7
- body, headless [may be M] (Be) — Hd

DW 9
+ flower [C?] (Be) — Bt

IX - DdW

DdW 22
+ section in zoology [C?] (Be) — An, Sc

either lateral half, entire

M+	˅bookkeeper sitting on high stool (<u>Be</u>)	H, Vo
+	landscape, modernistic [C?; V may be involved] (<u>Be</u>)	Ls
+	˅mirror reflection [C?; V?] (<u>Be</u>)	?
M+	˅woman gazing into mirror [V?] (<u>Be</u>)	H

several D indiscriminately

+	animals (<u>Be</u>)	A
-	animals (<u>Be</u>)	A

W, excluding D 4

-	thistle (<u>Be</u>)	Bt
M+	women, two, at tea table (<u>Be</u>)	H, Hh

Dd adjacent to D 2 including two prominent dots

+	face, cat's (<u>Be</u>)	Ad

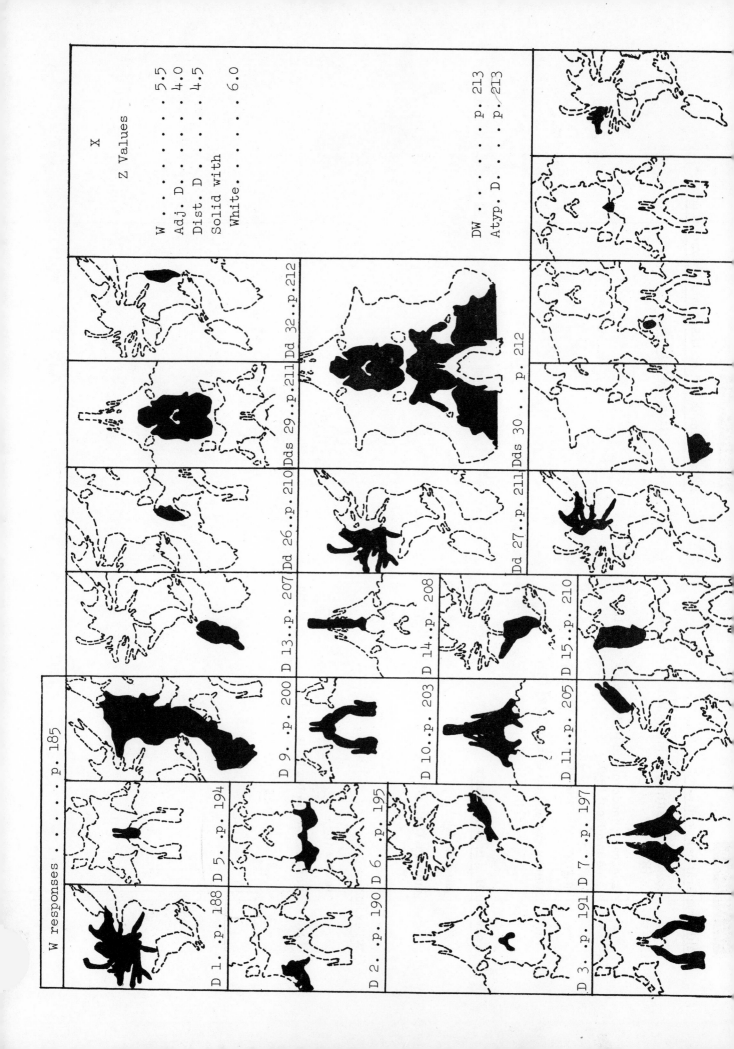

Note: Determination of color predominance (C, CF, FC) is difficult in many responses to this card without inquiry. The examiner's attention is directed to this necessity by the notation [C?]

Score	Content	Codes
-	alphabetical character, Chinese (Be)	Al
+	animals, all sorts [scored twice, + and -] (Be)	A
-	animals, all sorts [scored twice, + and -] (Be)	A
CF+	animals, sea (Ro)	A
+	aquarium [C?] (Be)	A?
M+	back, man's, bending over (Be)	Hd
+	banderilla [C?] (ᴿe)	Im
FC+	beetle collection, colored (Ro)	A
CF+	biology slide (Be)	Sc
+	botanic exhibit [C?] (Be)	Bt
-	butterfly [C?] (Be, Ob)	A
CF+	butterfly collection board (Bl)	A
FC+	caricature with yellow eyes [central yellow], nostrils [central blue] (Bl)	Hd, Art
CF	carnival, purest (Ro)	Rc
+	cartoon, Walt Disney [C?] (Be)	Art
+	chandelier [C?] (Be)	Hh
+	coat-of-arms [C?] (Be)	Art
-	cobweb (Be)	Na
CF.C	color blobs thrown with brush on cardboard (Bo)	Art
+	color on painter's palette (Be)	Art, Vo
C	colored sugar (Bl)	Fd
CF+	corals (Ro)	A
+	∧∨>< crabs, collection of [collection, i.e., perception of unified group, is +; if S had said simply crabs, one + and one - scoring would be necessary, since some of the details are + as crabs, other are -; C?] (Be)	A
-	∧∨>< crab collection [scored +, card in any position; see crabs under +; C?] (Be)	A
CF+	crockery pattern designed by handicraft (Ro)	Art
+	dance of life [may be M; C?] (Be)	Ab, H?
+	dance of the lower orders, floating in liquid air [C?] (Be)	Ab, A?
+	decoration, stage [C?] (Be)	Art
+	∨ design, anatomic [C?] (Be)	Art, Sc

X — W cont'd

Score	Response	Content
+	design, ceiling [in specifically named theater; C?] (Be)	Art
CF+	design on book of Middle Ages (Be)	Art
+	design, oriental [C?] (Be)	Art
+	design, wallpaper, for nursery [C?] (Be)	Art, Hh
-	drawing, dissected [C?] (Be)	Art, Sc
+	dream jumble [C?] (Be)	Ab
+	dream, Walt Disney [may be M; C?] (Be)	Ab
-	elephants, fairy-tale [C?] (Be)	A, My
+	emblem [C?] (Be)	Art
CF-	entrance to Heaven, clouds (Ro)	Cl, Rl
CF	explosion, rocket [because of the brilliant colors all going off in different directions] (Kl)	Fi
CF	expressionism, fantastic (Bl)	Art
+	˅fan [C?] (Be)	Pr
+	festival [may be M; C?] (Be)	Rc
+	figures, "Alice in Wonderland" [may be M; C?] (Be)	H?, A?
+	figures, tapestry [C?] (Be)	Art
+	˅fireworks [C?] (Be)	Fi, Rc
+	˅flower [C?] (Be)	Bt
FC+	flower [red], the flower leaves; inside the stamens, brush-edges, outside the leaves, gray middle; cup (Ro)	Bt
CF+	flower bunch (Bo)	Bt
CF	flowers (Ga)	Bt
+	flowers, bunch of, garden [C?] (Be)	Bt
+	˅fungus growth [C?] (Be)	Bt
CF+	initial A [red], with ornaments, as in handwritten books of ancient monks (Mu)	Al, Aq
+	insects [scored twice, + and - ; C?] (Be)	A
-	insects [scored twice, + and - ; C?] (Be)	A
+	menagerie [C?] (Be)	A
+	microscopic [C?] (Be)	Sc
CF+	microscopic stain (Be)	Sc
CF+	microscopic tissue (Be)	An, Sc
+	music [C?] (Be)	Ab, Mu
+	ocean bottom [C?] (Be)	Ls
+	˅orchid [C?] (Be)	Bt
FC-	organs, internal, man's (LU)	An
-	pagoda, oriental [C?] (Be)	Ar, Rl

+	work, kindergarten child's [C?] (Be)	Art
+	world's fair [C?] (Be)	Rc
+	worms [scored twice, + and -; C?] (Be)	A
-	worms [scored twice, + and -; C?] (Be)	A
+	zoo [C?] (Be)	A

C+	paint splashed by child (Be)	Art
CF	painting, expressionistic (Bo)	Art
CF	painting, impressionistic (Bo)	Art
+	painting, modern [C?] (Be)	Art
C+	palette, painter's, color on (Be)	Art, Vo
-	pliers (Be)	Im
F.M	pyramid, grand, with every animal supporting each other (Oe)	A
CF-	rose (Ro)	Bt
+	scene, kaleidoscope [C?] (Be)	Rc
+	scene, tropical [C?] (Be)	Ls
+	spring [C?] (Be)	Ab
C	stuff, colored (Ro)	Color
CF	system of parlor-philosopher (Bl)	Ab
-	tool, mechanical (Be)	Im
+	undersea life [C?] (Be)	A?, Bt?
+	vest, gaudy, with shirt [C?] (Be)	Cg, Pr
+	view, stereoptican [C?] (Be)	Rc
CF	wallpaper in a boarding house bed-room (Oe)	Art, Hh
M+	women and children going to circus [C?] (Be)	H, Rc

+	ameba in development [C?] (Be)	A, Sc
+	anemones, sea (Ro)	A
+	animal, deep-sea [C?] (Be)	A
+	animal, grotesque [C?] (Be)	A
+	animal, prehistoric [C?] (Be)	A, Sc
M+	animals, lively, dancing, foxes (Bl)	A
+	beetle [C?] (Be)	A
-	beetle with all the horns (Ro)	A
+	bouquet [C?] (Be)	Bt
+	branch (Be)	Bt
+	branches and stumps (Be)	Bt
+	bug with thousand legs [C?] (Be)	A
+	character from "Pilgrim's Progress" [may be M] (Be)	H
-	cloth, piece of [C?] (Be)	Hh
-	coral growing (Be)	A
FC+	cornflower (Ro)	Bt
+	^v CRAB [S] (Be, LU)	A
+	crab [s] (Ga, Ro)	A
+	creature waving something [C?] (Be)	A

+	CRUSTACEAN [S] (Be)	A
-	deadwood (Be)	Bt
-	dragon [s] (Be)	A, My
+	dragons (He)	A, My
+	elves [may be M] (Be)	H, My
+	endive (Be)	Bt
+	fern, sea [C?] (Be)	Bt
-	fish [C?] (Be)	A
-	fish, sea, with many legs (Bl)	A
-	flea [s] (Be)	A
+	flower [C?] (Be)	Bt
-	forest (Ro)	Bt
+	germ (Be)	Sc
M+	goblin with shadow [Y may be involved] (Be)	H, My
+	gremlin [s] [may be M] (Be)	H, My
+	hobgoblin [s] [may be M] (Be)	H, My
CF	ink, spilled (Bl)	Color
+	ink, upset [C?] (Be)	Color
+	ink-fishes (Ro)	A
+	insect [C?] (Be)	A

X — D 1 cont'd

	Content	Code
-	jellyfish [Y may be involved] (Be)	A
-	lady [may be M] (Be)	H
CF	lake, jagged, with inflowing streams (Ro)	Ls
+	landscape with high trees [V?] (Be)	Ls, Bt
+	larkspur [C?] (Be)	Bt
+	leaves, torn (Be)	Bt
+	lettuce (Be)	Bt
+	LOBSTER [C?] (Be)	A
-	lobsters (Bo)	A
+	magnified anything (Be)	?
+	magnified life [C?] (Be)	A?, Bt?
-	map, old [C?] (Be)	Ge
-	mask (Be)	Hd?, Rc?
+	octopus [es] [C?] (Be, Ga, Lu)	A
+	orchid [C?] (Be)	Bt
+	painting, ornamental [C?] (Be)	Art
+	pansies [C?] (Be)	Bt
M+	people, dancing (Be)	H
FC+	plants, sea (Ro)	Bt
+	roots, mass of (Be)	Bt

	Content	Code
+	scarab (Be)	Ay
+	scorpion (Be, Ro)	A
+	seaweed (Be)	Bt
-	shrubs (Ro)	Bt
+	snowflake (Be)	Na
+	SPIDER [S] (Be, Ga, LU)	A
+	spider [s] (Ro)	A
+	spider web (Be)	Na
FC+	sponges from sea bottom (Ro)	A
+	starfish (Be)	A
-	teakettle (Bl)	Hh
-	teapot (Be)	Hh
-	thigh in longitudinal section (Ro)	An, Sc
CF.TF	threads, blue wool, bunch of, soft looking (Kl)	Oj
+	turtle (He)	A
-	villages, farmers' (Lo)	Ru
M+	witches, two, one on broomstick (Be)	H, My

ATYPICAL
D 1, projecting Dd

	Content	Code
+	tree twigs (Be)	Bt

+	ameba [e] [Y may be involved] (Be)	A, Sc
-	angel [s] [may be M] (Be)	H, Rl
-	animal [s] [C?] (Be)	A
+	bird [s] [C?] (Be)	A
-	body, animal's, with baby bodies inside [Y may be involved] (Be)	A?, An?
+	buds (Bo)	Bt
+	butterfly [ies] [C?] (Be)	A
-	chair, easy (Be)	Hh
-	chicken [C?] (Be)	A
-	clown [s] [may be M; C?] (Be)	H
+	coat-of-arms [C?] (Be)	Art
+	deer [C?] (Be)	A
+	design [C?] (Be)	Art
+	doe [C?] (Be)	A
+	DOG (Be)	A
+	DOG, ESKIMO (Be)	A
+	dogs (Ga)	A
+	eagle, bald [C?] (Be)	A
+	eagle, golden [C?] (Be)	A
+	egg, fried [C?] (Be)	Fd

CF	egg, fried (Kl)	Fd
+	eyes, surprised [Y may be involved] (Be)	Hd?, Ad?
-	fish, with huge head and no body (Be)	Ad
+	flesh [C?] (Be)	Hd
+	flower petals [C?] (Be)	Bt
+	flowers [C?] (Be)	Bt
+	flowers, bell, two (Vi)	Bt
+	fox (LU)	A
-	goldfish [C?] (Be)	A
-	head with eye (Lo)	Hd?, Ad?
-	head, child's, in cloud (Ro)	Hd, Cl
-	head, rabbit's (Be)	Ad
-	jellyfish (Be)	A
+	lion [s] [C?] (Be, Ga, LU)	A
+	microscopic stains [C?] (Be)	Sc
-	milkweed pod [C?] (Be)	Bt
-	monkey [C?] (Be)	A
CF+	narcissus interior (Ro)	Bt
+	nuclei and cells [Y?; C?] (Be)	Sc
-	pitcher [s] (Be)	Hh

X — D 2 cont'd

+	POMERANIAN (Be)	A
+	POODLE (Be)	A
+	robin [s] (Be)	A
+	rooster (Lo)	A
-	rose, yellow [C?] (Be)	Bt
-	sea-horse (Be)	A
+	seal (Be)	A
+	sun, golden [C?] (Be)	As, Fi?
CF-	sun and moon (Ro)	As
CF+	sunflowers (Ro)	Bt
+	wings, butterfly's (LU)	Ad
M-	witches on broomstick (Be)	H, My
+	woodpecker [s] [C?] (Be)	A

ATYPICAL
D 2, with D 15

-	fish, yellow [C?] (Be)	A

+	antennae (LU)	Ad
+	apricot [C?] (Be)	Bt
-	bird [C?] (Be)	A
+	bladders, two pigs' (Vi)	A
+	bud [s] [C?] (Be, He)	Bt
-	buzzard (Be)	A
+	candelabra [C?] (Be)	Hh
+	castanets (LU)	Mu
+	cherries (Be)	Bt
M+	˅Chorus girl bowing (Be)	H
-	circlet [C?] (Be)	Pr
+	design [C?] (Be)	Art
M+	˅diver, high (Be)	H
-	ear-muff [C?] (Be)	Cg
+	˅eyes, two, and nose (Lo)	Hd?, Ad?
+	flower (He)	Bt
+	flower [s] on stem [C?] (Be)	Bt
+	governor, steam engine (Be)	Im
+	instrument to measure wind speed (Be)	Im
+	knocker [C?] (Be)	Im, Hh

X — D 3 cont'd

+	lavaliere [C?] (Be)	Pr	
+	lights, electric [C?] (Be)	Hh	
CF+	lights hanging from brass chandelier (Be)	Hh	
M+	man, suspended (Be)	H	
+	marigold [C?] (Be)	Bt	
-	necklace [C?] (Be)	Pr	
FC+	nuts, burst open, beech tree's (Mu)	Bt	
-	ovaries with fallopian tubes (Be)	An, Sex?	
M+	parachutists, landing (Be)	H, Tr	
+	pussywillows, two [C?] (Bo)	Bt	
+	seaweed [C?] (Be)	Bt	
+	seed [s] [C?] (Be, He)	Bt	
-	seed, male sex organ (Ro)	An, Sex?	
+	seed pod, maple tree's (Be)	Bt	
-	ship [s] at sea (Lo)	Ls, Tr	
+	sign, pawnbroker's [C?] (Be)	Im, Vo	
+	steeple, church (He)	Ar, Rl	
+	stethoscope (Be)	Im, Vo	
F.M	swing with little figure sitting on it (Kl)	H, Rc	
-	testicles (Be)	Hd, Sex	
+	Trinity symbol [C?] (Be)	Rl, Ab	
+	twig [C?] (Be)	Bt	
+	weathervane [C?] (Be)	Ar	
+	wishbone [C?] (Be, Ga)	An	
-	Y-shaped (Be)	Al	

X-D4

−	alligator [C?] (Be)	A
−	animal [C?] (Be)	A
−	animals, marine [C?] (Be)	A
+	animals, mythologic [C?] (Be)	A, My
−	bug [C?] (Be)	A
+	ᶺᵛcaterpillar [C?] (Be, Ga, Ro, Ve)	A
−	chicken (Be)	A
+	dragon [C?] (Be)	A, My
+	eel [s] [C?] (Be, Ve)	A
−	esophagus, dilated, with stomach (Be)	An, Sc
M−	figures, female, wrapped in veils [Y may be involved] (Be)	H, Cg
−	fish [es] (Be, Ro)	A
FC−	fish, green (Be)	A
+	ᵛhead, dragon's [C?] (Be)	Ad, My
+	ᵛhead, peacock's (Be)	Ad
−	head, person's, grotesque [may be M] (Be)	Hd
+	head and neck, bird's (Lo)	Ad
−	head and neck, swan's (Be)	Ad
−	hens sitting (Be)	A

+	horns, elk's (Be)	Ad
+	horns, ram's (Be)	Ad
−	horse, toy of rubber (Be)	A, Rc
+	insect [C?] (Be)	A
+	knight in chess (Be)	Rc
FC+	leaves on sprout (RO)	Bt
−	legs [may be M] (Be)	Hd
+	peacock [s] (Be)	A
FC+	petals on sprout (RO)	Bt
+	ᵛplant life, feathery [T?; Y?; C?] (Be)	Bt
−	porpoises (Be)	A
+	prawn [C?] (Be)	A
+	saxophone (Be)	Mu
+	ᶺᵛsea-horses [C?] (Be, Ve, Ro)	A
+	serpent [s] [C?] (Be)	A
+	serpents, sea (Ve)	A
−	snail [C?] (Be)	A
+	snake [s] [C?] (Be)	A
+	ᵛstamen, dusty [T?; Y?; C?] (Be)	Bt
−	swan (Be)	A

X — D 4 cont'd

-	swordfish (Be)	A
+	∨ tail, lyre bird's (Be)	A
+	tail, peacock's (Be)	A
-	tree [s] [C?] (Be)	Bt
-	turkey [s] (Be)	A
-	wings (Be)	Ad
M-	women, chattering (Be)	H
-	women, two [may be M] (Be)	H
M.FC(T)	women, two, going to mask ball; they are in conversation leaning toward each other. They wear long green velvet evening coats and long fluffy chiffon gowns (Kl)	H, Cg
+	∧>< worm [s] [C?] (Be, Ve, Ro)	A
-	wreath (He)	Bt

X — D 5

+	∨ angel [may be M] (Be)	H, Rl
+	bulb, electric (Bo)	Hh
+	BUNNY (Be)	Ad
+	∨ Christ on cross [may be M] (Be)	H, Rl
-	∨ Crucifix (Be)	Rl
M+	∨ diver (Be)	H
-	dog (Be)	A
+	face, animal's (Be)	Ad
+	face, creature's (Be)	Ad
-	face bones, elk's (Be)	An, Sc
+	∨ figure, little, with halo (Ro)	H, Rl
+	gargoyle (Be)	Art
-	genital, woman's (Ro)	Hd, Sex
+	head, animal's (Be)	Ad
-	head, devilish (Be)	Hd
-	head, donkey's (Be)	Ad
-	head, goat's (Be)	Ad
+	head, grasshopper's [C?] (Ga)	Ad
+	head, grotesque figure's (Be)	Hd
-	head, Indian's (Be)	Hd
-	head, insect's (Be)	Ad

+	head, person's (Be)	Hd
+	HEAD, RABBIT'S (Be, Ga)	Ad
-	head, snail's [C?] (Be)	Ad
+	head with two horns (Lo)	Ad
-	∨insect (Be)	A
-	labia (Be)	Hd, Sex
-	lobster (Be)	A
M+	∨man, diving (Be)	H
M+	∨man, doing calisthenics, with halo (Be)	H, Rl
M+	∨man, hanging on to two things, suspended in air (Be)	H
+	mask (Be)	Hd?, Rc?
M+	∨person on a swing (Be)	H, Rc
-	pliers (Be)	Im
-	wrench (Be)	Im

M+	∨angels, two, on cliff [V may be involved] (Be)	H, Ls
+	animal (Be)	A
FC-	animal from coat-of-arms (Ro)	A, Art
-	ape [s] [Y may be involved] (Be)	A
+	∧∨birds [C?] (Be)	A
+	bluebird [C?] (Be)	A
+	bone [s], hip (Be)	An
+	bones, pelvic (Be, Ga)	An
-	bulls, two little (Ro)	A
+	chicken quartered for broiling (Be)	Ad
-	clouds [Y and T may be involved] (Be)	Cl
+	doll [C?] (Be)	H, Rc
M.FC	>Donald Duck whistling walking along gaily. Has a blue jacket and a fluffy blue shirt on (Kl)	A, Cg
+	doves [C?] (Be)	A
+	duck [s] [C?] (Be)	A
-	<face, hook-nosed (Be)	Hd
+	∨ghosts [Y may be involved; may be M] (Be)	H

M+	∨gods, Roman, spanning world (Be)	H, My
-	gorilla [Y may be involved] (Be)	A
-	hands [may be M] (Be)	Hd
+	∨head (Lo)	Hd
+	head [s], animal's (Be, LU)	Ad
+	∧∨head, dog's (Be)	Ad
+	head, elephant's (Be)	Ad
+	head, elephant's, very young (Ro)	Ad
+	heads, two foxes', in a ravine (Ro)	Ad, Ls
+	heads, two pigs' (Ro)	Ad
-	lakes [C?] (LU)	Ls
C	lakes (LU)	Ls
+	lungs (Du)	An
-	map of United States [C?] (Be)	Ge
M+	men shaking hands (Be)	H
M+	men, two, fat, hanging onto rocks with one hand, and reaching a towel with the other (Be)	H, Ls
M+	∨men, two, holding themselves over a precipice (Ro)	H, Ls
M+	∨men, two, on rocks; one wants to help the other cross over (Bo)	H, Ls

-	moose (Be)	A
-	ostrich [es] [C?] (Be)	A
M+	people in motion (Ga)	H
+	∨people, two [may be M] (Be)	H
M+	∨performers on stage (Be)	H
-	pigs [C or Y may be involved] (Be)	A
-	pipe, smoking (Be)	Oj
-	pitcher [C?] (Be)	Hh
-	storks (Be)	A
-	turkey (Be)	A
+	vertebra (Mu)	An
-	vise (Be)	Im

ATYPICAL
D 6, both, as unit

-	bat [C?] (Be)	A
+	bones, skeletal (Be)	A
+	bottom, human skeleton (Be)	An
+	bridge (Be)	Ar
+	cartilage, held together [Y may be involved] (Be)	An
+	pelvis (Be)	An

+	animal [s], leaping [C?] (Be)	A
M?	animal running (Ga)	A
+	ant [s] [C?] (Be)	A
M+	back floater [s] (Be)	H, Rc
+	beetle [s] [C?] (Be, Ro)	A
-	bird [s] (Be)	A
+	bird (LU)	A
+	birds with long necks (Ro)	A
+	ᐱᐯ bug [s] [C?] (Be)	A
-	cat (Be)	A
FC+	chicken, plucked, which is being fried (Mu)	Fd
-	chicken, skinned (Be)	A
+	ᐯ cocoon on branch [C?] (Be)	Ad, Bt
-	cow (Be)	A
+	crabs (Be)	A
-	crabs (Ro)	A
M+	creature, primitive, walking (Ro)	A
+	cricket [C?] (Be)	A
+	deer [C?] (Be)	A
-	deer (Ro)	A
M	deer jumping (Ga)	A
-	dog [C?] (Be)	A
-	ducks, butchered (Be)	A
+	fish, sea (Be)	A
-	flea (Be)	A
-	frog (Be)	A
-	ᐯ goblins, horrible [may be M] (Be)	H, My
+	grasshopper [C?] (Be, Bl)	A
-	grouse (Be)	A
+	insect [C?] (Be)	A
+	kangaroo [C?] (Be)	A
-	kangaroo, young (Ro)	A
-	kidney with ureter (Be)	An
+	larva (LU)	Ad
-	lobster (LU)	A
+	may-bug (LU)	A
FC+	mice, two little (Ro)	A
+	ᐱᐯ< mouse [C?] (Be)	A
-	mouse-like (Ro)	A
+	nest in branches (Be)	Na, Bt
-	nests (Ro)	Na

−	owl [C?] (Be)	A
+	pod [C?] (Be)	Bt
+	pods, milkweed [C?] (Be)	Bt
+	⌄foot, bulbous [C?] (Be)	Bt
+	roots, potato [C?] (Be)	Bt
−	sea-horses [C?] (Be)	A
+	sea-moss, rubbery [T?; Y?; C?] (Be)	Bt
−	⌃sea-urchin [C?] (Be)	A
	⌄skull (Be)	An
−	spider [s] [C?] (Be)	A
−	squirrel [C?] (Be, Lo)	A
−	stork (Be, Bl)	A
+	storks, two (Ro)	A
+	tree section with roots and dirt [C?] (Be)	Bt
+	turtle [C?] (Be)	A
−	worm [s] [C?] (Be)	A

+	animal [s] [C?] (Be, He)	A
−	animals, unspecified (Ro)	A
−	ants [C?] (Be)	A
−	bat [s] with wings folded [C?] (Be)	A
−	bee [s] (Be)	A
+	beetle [s] [C?] (Be)	A
+	buffalo [C?] (Be)	A
+	bug [s] [C?] (Be, He)	A
−	bulls [C?] (Be)	A
−	bunnies [C?] (Be)	A
−	chickens (Be)	A
+	chipmunk [C?] (Be)	A
−	crab (Be)	A
+	crawfish (He)	A
+	creatures, monstrous, two [may be M] (Be)	H?, A?
+	creatures, weird [may be M] (Be)	H?, A?
−	dogs (Be)	A
+	dragon (Be)	A, My
+	⌄faces, grotesque [may be M] (Be)	Hd
+	⌄figures, fairy-tale [may be M] (Be)	H, My

-	fish [C?] (Be)	A	
+	flea [s] [C?] (Be)	A	
-	fleas (Ro)	A	
-	flower [s] (Be)	Bt	
-	frog [s] (Be)	A	
+	gargoyle (Be)	Art	
-	goat [C?] (Be)	A	
M+	gods, Egyptian, dancing (Be)	H, My	
+	gryphon (Be)	A, My	
-	hares (Ro)	A	
+	hares, two young (Bo)	A	
-	head, grasshopper's [C?] (Be)	Ad	
+	heads, human [may be M] (Be)	Hd	
+	heads, two Indians' (Ro)	Hd	
-	hens (Be)	A	
+	humans, two [may be M] (Be)	H	
+	insects [C?] (Be, He)	A	
-	kidney [s] (Be)	An	
+	kitten [s] (Be)	A	
-	lion (Be)	A	

-	lobster (Be)	A	
+	mice, field [C?] (Be)	A	
+	mice, two, standing on hind legs (Ro)	A	
+	molds, furry [T?; Y?; C?] (Be)	Bt	
-	∨ ovary (Be)	An, Sex	
-	parakeet [s] (Be)	A	
-	parrots (Be)	A	
M+	people, dancing (Be)	H	
+	people, two [may be M] (Be)	H	
-	pheasants (Be)	A	
-	porcupines (Be)	A	
+	pollywog (Be)	A	
+	profile [person, Jewish] (Ro)	Hd	
-	rabbits [C?] (Be)	A	
+	rats [C?] (Be)	A	
+	rodents [C?] (Be)	A	
-	sea-leopard (Be)	A	
-	skeleton, piece of (Be)	An	
-	smoke [Y?] (Be)	Fi	
-	∧∨ spider [s] [C?] (Be)	A	

X ──D 8 cont'd

+	spiders (He)	A
+	squirrels [C?] (Be)	A
+	squirrels, two, bowing [may be M] (Bl)	A
-	testicles (Be)	Hd, Sex
-	toads (Ro)	A
-	turtle [s] [C?] (Be)	A
-	turtles (He)	A
+	unicorn (Be)	A, My
-	woodchucks [C?] (Be)	A

ATYPICAL
Dd projecting from D 8

M-	person, arms up, belssing or ask-ing for blessing (Be)	Hd

-	ameboid mass [C?; Y?] (Be)	A, Sc
+	animals in fairy tales (Be)	A, My
-	arches (Be)	Ar
+	attachment, Christmas tree [C?] (Be)	Art, Rc
-	bear (Be)	A
+	blood spots [C?] (Be)	Blood
-	bones, buttocks (Vi)	An, Sex
M+	boxers, two (Be)	H, Rc
+	boy [may be M] (Be)	H
+	California [C?] (Be)	Ge
-	caterpillar [C?] (Be)	A
+	caterpillar, magnified [Y?; C?] (Be)	A
+	child [ren] [may be M] (Be)	H
M+	children, two, leaning toward each other; they have very big feet (Be)	H
+	cliff [V?] (Be)	Ls
+	clouds [Y?; T?] (Be)	Cl
+	coastline [C?; Y?] (Be)	Ls
+	coral, pink [C?] (Be)	Na
+	cowboy [may be M] (Be)	H

+	map of Italy [C?] (Be)	Ge
C	meat, tainted (Be)	Fd
+	men, two [may be M] (Be)	H
+	monsters, marine [C?] (Be)	A
FV+	mountain [s] (Be, Ga)	Ls
FV+	mountain chain [Y?] (Be)	Ls
CF	mountains in the red of the setting sun (Ro)	Ls
FC+	mountains with sunlight on them (Lo)	Ls
FV+	mountainside [Y?] (Be)	Ls
-	Netherlands [C?] (Be)	Ge
-	ocean [C?; Y?] (Be)	Ls
M+	people leaning backward (Be)	H
+	people, two [may be M] (Be)	H
+	∧∨ petals [C?] (Be)	Bt
-	porpoises (Be)	A
+	priests, headless [may be M] (Be)	Hd, Rl
M+	⟩ roller coaster with riders (Be)	H, Rc
+	sea-horse (Be)	A
+	seashore [C?] (Be)	Ls
+	shore line [C?] (Be)	Ls

A B 5 cont'd

+	design on man's coat [both D 9 as unit; C?] (Be)	Art, Cg
+	divers, sea [may be M] (Be)	H
-	dolphin (Be)	A
+	figure, human, any [may be M] (Be)	H
-	figure, lady's, without head (Ml)	Hd
M+	figures, female, wrapped in veil [Y?; T?] (Be)	H, Cg
+	figures, male [may be M] (Be)	H
+	figures, two, marching, without heads (Ro)	Hd
+	fire and smoke [C?; Y?] (Be)	Fi
+	flame [C?] (Be)	Fi
CF-	flesh (Ro)	Hd
-	insects reared to fight (Be)	A
CF	inside, female genital (Ro)	An, Sex
+	jesters, court [may be M; C?] (Be)	H
C	love (Ro)	Ab
M+	lovers, leaning toward each other, held apart by the blue and they are pushing against it (Be)	H
M+	man hanging in space (Be)	H
+	map [C?; Y?] (Be)	Ge

X — D 9 cont'd

CF-	sides, human body (Ro)	Hd
CF+	smoke, red, from fireplace (Du)	Fi
+	snow suit (Be)	Cg
M+	soldiers, two, moving forward in a grenade attack and looking back on a hand-grenade, which they are about to throw (Mu)	H, Im
+	∨stage curtains opened [both D 9 as unit; C?] (Be)	Rc
-	tree trunk (Be)	Bt
-	ulcerated region [C?] (Be)	An
+	Wizard of Oz [may be M; C?] (Be)	H
M+	woman, irate, in evening dress [C?] (Be)	H, Cg
-	women (Ro)	H
+	women, Japanese [may be M; C?] (Be)	H
-	women, two, dancing, without heads (Du)	Hd
M+	workmen drilling (Be)	H, Vo
-	worm [C?] (Be)	A

ATYPICAL
D 9, edge Dd

+	land ploughed over [Y?] (Be)	Ls, Ru

+	map of coast [C?; Y?] (Be)	Ge

D 9, both, as unit

+	archway [V may be involved] (Be)	Ar
+	canyon [V may be involved] (Be)	Ls
-	chair, prone (Be)	Hh
-	gray matter [Y?] (Be)	An
+	∨mountains with valley between [V?] (Be)	Ls

D 9, with D 6

M+	humans holding hands (Be)	H

D 9, both, with D 6, D 11

+	flower, any [C?] (Be)	Bt
+	letter "A", illuminated [C?] (Be)	Al
-	pelvis (Be)	An

D 9, with D 8

+	monsters (Be)	A?, H?

ATYPICAL
D 9, with D 11

M-	bags of cement being wheeled (Be)	H, Vo	
-	bone, animal's jaw (Be)	An	
-	chest [C?] (Be)	An	
M+	firemen, drunk, knocking against pole [upper gray] (Ro)	H	
+	˅ flower [C?] (Be)	Bt	
-	necklace design [C?] (Be)	Art, Pr	
C.Y.	˃ sunset extending quite far, covering the sky. Here it is getting darker already and from here [central gray] night moves in (Bi)	Ls	
FC	throat and lungs (LU)	An	
M+	women with gray heads, marching toward each other (Ro)	H	

+	˅ antlers (Bl)	Ad
-	bird (Be)	A
-	candle holder (Be)	Hh
-	comb, old-fashioned (Be)	Pr
-	creature (Be)	A?, H?
-	Cross (Be)	Rl
+	design [C?] (Be)	Art
+	design, art, for building [C?] (Be)	Art
-	devilfish (Be)	A
-	dog (Be)	A
+	door knocker (Be)	Hh
-	flower [C?] (Be)	Bt
-	fountain (Be)	Ls
-	gargoyle from which two long pigtails are hanging down (Ob)	Hd, Art
+	haircomb, modern, with ornament (Ro)	Pr
+	hare (Ro)	A
-	harness for horse (Be)	Im
+	harp (LU)	Mu
+	head, animal's as in ancient design [C?] (Be)	Ad, Art

-	head, bull's (Be)	Ad
+	head, rabbit's (Ro)	Ad
+	head, ram's (Be)	Ad
+	head, sea-horse's, ornament of (Bl)	Ad, Art
-	headdress (Be)	Pr
+	horns, animal's (Be)	Ad
-	horseshoe (Be)	Im
-	insect [C?] (Be)	A
FC+	lamp, electric, green, hanging (Mu)	Hh
-	light, electric, hanging from ceiling (Be)	Hh
+	˅lyre (Be)	Mu
+	magnet (Ro)	Im
M+	˅man, flying (Be)	H
+	˅man with halo and wings [may be M] (Be)	H, Rl
+	music holder for brass instrument (Bo)	Mu
+	music stand (Be)	Mu
-	octopus (Be)	A
M+	parachutist (Be)	H
-	praying-mantis [C?] (Be)	A
FC+	priest with decorative ornament on head, in loose, green cloak (Ro)	H, Rl
+	saint, little, with two grotesque, long, outstretched arms (Du)	H, Rl
-	scene, marine [C?] (Be)	Ls
+	section, longitudinal, through a blossom (Bo)	Bt
+	snake with two bodies [C?] (Be)	A
-	˅stamen [C?] (Be)	Bt
-	U shape (Be)	Al
-	weasels, two (Ro)	A
-	wishbone (Be)	An
+	worm on fish hook [C?] (Be)	A, Rc
+	wreath [C?] (Be)	Bt

+	animals supporting tube [may be M; C?] (Be)	A
+	animals, two (LU)	A
-	anteater [C?] (Be)	A
+	art piece, oriental [C?] (Be)	Art
+	backbone and attached bones (Be)	An
+	bark, plant [C?] (Be)	Bt
+	beavers gnawing at tree [C?] (Be)	A, Bt
+	beetles, sucking on joint of flower stem (Mu)	A, Bt
-	body, human, part of (Be)	Hd
M	bugs, two, little, holding something up, deeply in a diplomatic discussion (Kl)	A
+	chandelier (Be)	Hh
-	cross section, nervous system (Be)	An, Sc
M+	dancers around Maypole (Be)	H, Rc
+	Eiffel Tower [C?] (Be)	Ar
-	fireplace [C?] (Be)	Ar
+	flower (Be)	Bt
+	flower-cup (Bo)	Bt
+	headgear on Buddha [C?] (Be)	Cg, Rl

-	implement for snipping pears from trees (Be)	Im
+	insect leaning against pole [may be M] (Be)	A
+	insects, two (LU)	A
-	intestines (Be)	An
+	lamp, electric, hanging (Be)	Hh
+	lobster (LU)	A
+	marionettes on string [may be M] (Be)	H, Rc
M+	men on telephone pole (Be)	H
-	mermaid (Ro)	H, My
+	mice, field, gnawing on stalk [C?] (Be)	A, Bt
-	mirage (Be)	Ab
+	mistletoe (Be)	Bt
-	Palestine [C?] (Be)	Ge
-	phallus with testicles (Be)	Hd, Sex
-	picture of lung (Bo)	Art, An
M+	pole supported by two people (Be)	H, Im
+	rats strung up on post [C?] (Be)	A
M+	savages dancing around tree (Be)	H, Bt

-	⌄shellfish [C?] (Be)	A
+	⌄skeleton, animal's, with fang (Lo)	An
+	skull, animal's (Ro)	An
-	skull, steer's (Be)	An
+	statue (Be)	Art
+	stem, bamboo, with roots (Be)	Bt
+	⌃stem, flower (Be)	Bt
+	toy stick with bells (Be)	Rc, Mu
+	transformers on telephone pole [C?] (Be)	Im
-	trachea and lungs (Be)	An
+	⌄tree (Be)	Bt
-	tree (Be)	Bt
-	⌄universal on automobile (Be)	Im, Tr
CF	woods, young, where the bushes are (Lo)	Bt
-	x-ray, centipede [Y?] (Be)	An

-	angel [may be M] (Be)	H, Rl
-	animal [s] (Be)	A
-	ax (Be)	Im
-	bird (Be)	A
-	broom (Be)	Im, Hh
-	bud [C?] (Be)	Bt
-	bug [s] [C?] (Be)	A
+	bull charging (Be)	A
-	cat (Be)	A
-	caterpillar [C?] (Be)	A
+	chrysalis (LU)	A
-	claw (Be)	Ad
-	coral (Be)	A
+	cow jumping (Be)	A
-	dog (Be)	A
-	fan [C?] (Be)	Pr
+	fish [C?] (Be)	A
+	fish, under side of (Lo)	Ad
-	frog [C?] (Be)	A
-	grasshopper [C?] (Be)	A
FC	grasshopper, green, jumping (Kl)	A

−	horseshoe (Be)	Im
−	Iceland [C?] (Be)	Ge
+	lamb (Be)	A
+	leaf [C?] (Be, He)	Bt
−	map of island [C?] (Be)	Ge
−	mouse (Be)	A
−	parrot [C?] (Be)	A
−	plume, soldier's [C?] (Be)	Pr
−	rock [C?] (Be)	Ls
−	scarab [s] worshiping [C?] (Be)	Ay, Rl
−	seed [C?] (Be)	Bt
+	SHEEP (Be)	A
+	sheep, little, lying (Ro)	A
−	snow bank [Y may be involved] (Be)	Na
−	tree [C?] (Be)	Bt
C	turf to be cut (Ro)	Ls
+	unicorn (Be)	A, My
+	whale, small (Be)	A
CF.TF	wool, green, bunch of, wrapped around stick (Kl)	Hh

+	animal [C?] (Be, Lo)	A
+	bear [C?] (Be)	A
+	bear, picture of (Ob)	A, Art
−	bird [C?] (Be)	A
+	buffalo [C?] (Be)	A
+	bull, picture of (Ob)	A, Art
−	bunny (Be)	A
−	cat (Be)	A
−	chicken, roast [C?] (Be)	A, Fd
+	cloud [s] [C?; Y?; T?] (Be, LU)	Cl
CF.Y	cloud, evening (Kl)	Cl
+	daub of paint [C?] (Be)	Art
+	dog, any (Be)	A
+	dog lying down [C?] (Ga)	A
+	face, dog's [C?] (Be)	Ad
−	fish with mouth open [C?] (Be)	A
−	flower [C?] (Be)	Bt
+	island (He)	Ge
CF+	island of Corsica [C?] (Be)	Ge
	islands, brown (Be)	Ge
+	leaf [C?] (Be)	Bt

X — 13 cont'd

+	lion (Lo)		A
+	lion lying down [C?] (Be)		A
-	man [may be M] (Be)		H
+	mold, insect [C?; Y?; T?] (Be)		A
FC-	mountain covered with woods (Lo)		Ls, Bt
-	New Zealand [C?] (Be)		Ge
-	porpoise (Be)		A
-	rabbit (Be)		A
FC-	ram, brown, running (Be)		A
+	rust on something (He)		Oj
-	sheep (Be)		A
+	slug [s] [C?] (Be)		A
-	snail [C?] (Be)		A
+	spaniel [C?] (Be)		A
-	tonsil [s] (Be)		An
-	turkey, roast [C?] (Be)		A, Fd
-	whale (Be)		A

-	arrow (Be)	Im
+	backbone (Ga)	An
+	baton (Be)	Mu
-	bone (Be)	An
+	branch [C?] (Be)	Bt
+	candle (Be)	Hh
+	candle-holder (Be)	Hh
+	cannon [C?] (Be)	Im
FT	chimney, glass, delicate, tall, of old-fashioned kerosene lamp (Kl)	Hh
-	cigar [C?] (Be)	Oj
-	cord, spinal part (Be)	An
-	dissection, piece of (Be)	An
-	esophagus, upper (Du)	An
+	face in mirror, long and thin [may be M] (Be)	Hd
+	flashlight (Be)	Im
+	Jehovah [may be M] (Be)	H, Rl
-	key (Be)	Im
-	knife in sheath (Be)	Im
+	lamp-post [C?] (Be)	Ls

+	vase (<u>Be</u>)	Hh
+	vegetation (<u>Be</u>)	Bt
+	vertebral column (<u>Vi</u>)	An
+	windpipe (<u>Lo</u>)	An
+	woman, headless [may be M] (<u>Be</u>)	Hd
M+	woman, nude, standing with hands up (<u>Be</u>)	H

+	log [C?] (<u>Be</u>)	Bt
M+	man in tall hat for funeral [C?] (<u>Be</u>)	H, Dh
+	man with long face [may be M] (<u>Be</u>)	H
+	mast, ship's (<u>Ro</u>)	Tr
+	Maypole (<u>Be</u>)	Rc
-	monkey [s] [C?] (<u>Be</u>)	A
+	phallus (<u>Be</u>)	Hd, Sex
-	pier, very big, for sea ships (<u>Lo</u>)	Ls
+	pipe, piece of [C?] (<u>Be</u>)	Oj
-	pistil, Easter lily [C?] (<u>Be</u>)	Bt
+	pole [C?] (<u>Be</u>)	Im
+	pole, flag [C?] (<u>Be</u>)	Im
-	snout (<u>Be</u>)	Ad
+	stalk [C?] (<u>Be</u>)	Bt
+	test tube (<u>Be</u>)	Im, Sc
+	thermometer (<u>Be</u>)	Im
+	throat interior (<u>Be</u>)	An
+	tree [C?] (<u>Be</u>)	Bt
+	tree stem [C?] (<u>Be</u>)	Bt
-	urethra (<u>Be</u>)	An

X - D 15

+	ameba (Be)	A, Sc
+	bird [C?] (Be)	A
+	bud [C?] (Be)	Bt
-	canary [C?] (Be)	A
+	cloud across sunrise [C?; Y?; T?] • (Be)	Cl, Ls
CF-	comets, two, with tails (Bo)	As
-	fish (Be)	A
+	flower [C?] (Be, Ga)	Bt
-	island [C?] (Be)	Ls
CF-	kidney (Ro)	An
FC+	parrot (Lo)	A
M+	rug, magic, with people on it [C?; Y?] (Be)	My, H
FC.FT	snapdragon, yellow, with delicate petals (Ki)	Bt
+	South America (RO)	Ge
CF+	spot, dirt (Be)	Spot

X - Dd 25

-	dog (Be)	A
+	doll, rag [C?; may be M] (Be)	H, Rc
+	face [may be M] (Be)	Hd
+	France (He)	Ge
FT	head, frog's, eyes sticking out on top, the veining and rough skin texture (Ki)	Ad
+	head, girl's [may be M] (Be)	Hd
-	head, sea-horse's (Ro)	Ad

X - Dd 26

+	face, funny [may be M] (Be)	Hd
+	man, old, Semitic [may be M] (Be)	H
+	profile, man's [may be M] (Be)	Hd

ATYPICAL
Dd 26 with D 6

M+	chef, barbecuing a chicken (Be)	H, A

Note: Beck advises that + or - judgments for this Dds remain subjective because too few responses have been recorded. Safe scoring is F, without + or -. He offers some of his subjective scorings.

M+	clown on trapeze [C?] (Be)	H, Rc
+	goblin [may be M] (Be)	H, My
+	horse (Be)	A
+	men [may be M] (Be)	H
-	vulture [s] (Be)	A

X - Dd 28

+	cat sitting, reaching for something (Be)	A
M+	clown, tattered, sitting on trapeze [C?] (Be)	H, Rc
+	head, horse's (Be)	Ad
+	horses, chess (Be)	Ad, Rc
+	monkey (Be)	A
-	sea-horses (Be)	A

ATYPICAL
Dd 28, with D 12

-	cat on limb of tree (Be)	A, Bt
-	dusting broom (Be)	Im, Hh

+	animal, sea (Ro)	A
-	doggie (Be)	A
-	face [may be M] (Be)	Hd
+	head (Lo)	Hd
+	lake (He)	Ls
-	man, double-faced [may be M] (Be)	Hd
-	papoose [may be M] (Be)	H
+	perfume bottle with atomizer (Ro)	Pr
-	pup (Be)	A

ATYPICAL
Dds 29, with D 11

+	fan, Japanese (Be)	Pr
-	tennis racket (Be)	Im, Rc
-	violin (Be)	Mu

X - Dds 30

−	body, part of (Be)	Hd
+	canal with locks [V?] (Be)	Ls
+	Eiffel Tower (He)	Ar
F	ˇface (Kl)	Hd
FY	path of garden and bushes on the sides; in the distance a temple [the shading of the temple shows that it is far away] (Kl)	Ls
FY.FV	road, park; the dark hue of the trees [shaded parts of the gray above] and in the middle a path stretching a long, long way (Ro)	Ls
−	skeleton (Be)	An

X - Dd 31

−	cat (Be)	A
+	face [may be M] (Be)	Hd

X - Dd 32

+	face, Al Smith's [may be M] (Be)	Hd
+	face, funny [may be M] (Be)	Hd
+	face, person's (He)	Hd
+	ˇhead (Mu)	Hd
+	ˇhead, human (Ob)	Hd

X - Dd 33

+	acorns (Be)	Bt
+	heads, babies' [may be M] (Be)	Hd
−	tooth (Be)	Hd?, Ad?
+	walnut [C?] (Be)	Bt

D indiscriminately (usually several included, but not W)

Note: + or − scoring is subjective.

−	ball (Be)	Rc	
−	boat (Be)	Tr	
−	bone (Be)	An	
−	gate [V may be involved] (Be)	Ar	
−	head, skeleton (Be)	An	
−	horns, animal's (Be)	Ad	
−	muff (Be)	Cg	
−	top of woman's bathing suit (Be)	Cg	

X - Dd 35

+	landscape in perspective [V?] (Be)	Ls	

X - DW

−	marine animal remains [sundry D; C?] (Be)	Ad	

M	acrobats [C?] (Be)	H
F	animals [C?] (Be)	A
F	animals, prehistoric [C?] (Be)	A, Sc
F	beetles and crabs [C?] (Be)	A
F	birds [C?] (Be)	A
F	buds [C?] (Be)	Bt
F	coat-of-arms [C?] (Be)	Art
F	flowers [C?] (Be)	Bt
F	insects [C?] (Be)	A
F	marine growths [C?] (Be)	A?, Bt?
F	mirror objects [C?; V?; Y?] (Be)	Oj
F	sea bottom [C?] (Be)	Ls
F	sea matter [C?] (Be)	A?, Bt?
F	sea monsters [C?] (Be)	A
F	⌄spots on butterfly wings [C?] (Be)	Ad
F	tissue, body, under microscope [C?] (Be)	An, Sc
F	worms [C?] (Be)	A

213

X — ATYPICAL D cont'd

W, excluding D 1

+   flower, any [C?] (Be)   Bt

+   orchid [C?] (Be)   Bt

W, excluding D 10, D 11

+   Christmas card, modernistic [C?] (Be)   Art, Rc